ADVANCE PRAISE FOR *HOW TO MAKE A SLAVE*

"These aren't essays. This is hypnosis, a spell of enchantment cast over the reader by a masterful writer whose crystal-clear vision is not only original but revelatory. I laughed out loud, nodded at Jerald Walker's delivery of so much truth, and just shook my head at how gracefully he achieves so much so quickly in every piece in *How to Make a Slave*. All I can say is, 'Wow.' And you can't just consume one; you'll find yourself gobbling down every essay here and hungering for more. No one—absolutely no one—I've read is writing better than Jerald Walker about race, being black, and the depths and complexities of our humanity."

—Charles Johnson, author of *Middle Passage*, winner of the National Book Award

"Ignited by the everyday sparks of racial conflict—whether on a college campus or in an aisle at Whole Foods—these extraordinarily candid essays crackle with humor and dramatic tension. As 'race stories,' they also add a creative and subtle twist to an issue too often expressed in predictable polemics. This new collection establishes Jerald Walker as truly one of the most gifted essayists of our time."

—Robert Atwan, Series Editor, *Best American Essays*

"I've been waiting for this, the first collection of essays by one of our best essayists, for years. Jerald Walker's *How to Make a Slave* is notable for its persistence of vision. These essays are relentlessly humane even as they stare into America's split, racist heart. And like America and Americans, this book is both funny and fucked up, and neither can exist without the other."

—Ander Monson, author of *I Will Take the Answer*

"This piercing and restless collection slices through this country's agitated racial landscape with the tenacity of a thunderbolt. Walker manages to be all of us—we are all the college English department's pet token, we are all the potential Whole Foods crime wave, we are all the Negro middle American agonizing over a return trip to the implosive inner city from whence we came. These fresh, revelatory snippets of black life deserve a rollicking collective *Amen!* and an audience of both the converted and the curious."

—Patricia Smith, author of *Incendiary Art*

"If there is a book you need to read as our country is about to devour itself, it is *How to Make a Slave*. Walker's sharp voice cuts through the social malaise of our culture, delivering intimate moments of his life—from a boy in South Chicago to a young student writer trying to find voice amid a myriad of black stereotypes to a father raising two boys in a divided country. These essays enlighten us through depth and complexity of thought and the veracity of experience."

—Ira Sukrungruang, author of *Buddha's Dog and Other Meditations*

HOW TO MAKE A SLAVE

21ST CENTURY ESSAYS
David Lazar and Patrick Madden, Series Editors

HOW TO
MAKE A SLAVE
AND OTHER ESSAYS

Jerald Walker

MAD CREEK BOOKS, AN IMPRINT OF
THE OHIO STATE UNIVERSITY PRESS
COLUMBUS

Copyright © 2020 by Jerald Walker.

All rights reserved.

Published by Mad Creek Books, an imprint of The Ohio State University Press.

Library of Congress Cataloging-in-Publication Data

Names: Walker, Jerald, author.

Title: How to make a slave and other essays / Jerald Walker.

Other titles: 21st century essays.

Description: Columbus : Mad Creek Books, an imprint of The Ohio State
    University Press, [2020] | Series: 21st century essays | Summary: "Personal
    essays exploring identity, family, and community through the prism of
    race and black culture. Confronts the medical profession's racial biases,
    shopping while black at Whole Foods, the legacy of Michael Jackson,
    raising black boys, haircuts that scare white people, racial profiling, and
    growing up in Southside Chicago"—Provided by publisher.

Identifiers: LCCN 2020007415 | ISBN 9780814255995 (paperback) | ISBN
    081425599X (paperback) | ISBN 9780814278215 (ebook) | ISBN
    0814278213 (ebook)

Subjects: LCSH: Walker, Jerald. | African Americans—Race identity. | Race
    discrimination. | Families. | American essays—21st century.

Classification: LCC PS3623.A35938 A6 2020 | DDC 305.896—dc23

LC record available at https://lccn.loc.gov/2020007415

Cover design by Amanda Weiss

Text design by Juliet Williams

Type set in ITC New Baskerville

in memory of
James Alan McPherson

CONTENTS

How to Make a Slave   1

Dragon Slayers   7

Before Grief   16

Inauguration   21

Kaleshion   29

The Heritage Room   36

Unprepared   42

Feeding Pigeons   49

Breathe   56

The Heart   63

Balling   68

Testimony   75

Smoke   82

Wars   89

Simple   94

The Designated Driver   100

Strippers 108

Thieves 116

Once More to the Ghetto 120

Race Stories 136

Advice to a Family Man 142

Acknowledgments *149*

HOW TO MAKE A SLAVE

Gather scissors, construction paper, crayons, popsicle sticks, and glue. Take them to the den where your thirteen-year-old sister sits at the table thumbing through your schoolbook on black history. Smile when she notices you and turns to the pre-marked page with a photo of Frederick Douglass. It's one from his later years, when his Afro was white. Realize you need cotton balls. Leave and return with them in a moment to see that your sister has already cut from the construction paper a circle that will serve as Douglass's head. Start gluing the popsicle sticks together to make his body. As you work silently, your sister tells you basic facts about slavery and abolition that you will present to your class. You'll end the presentation by saying with passion that Frederick Douglass is your hero, which will not be true because you are only ten and the things you are learning about black history make it difficult to feel good about his life, and sometimes yours.

But feel good about the beating he gave his master. Your classmates feel good about it too. They cheer when you describe it, as they cheered seconds earlier when you recited Douglass's famous line: *You have seen how a man was made a slave; you shall see how a slave was made a man.* "I wouldn't have taken that stuff either," one of your class-mates says after school. Forget his name in a few years but remember his skin was so dark that you and your friends had no choice but to call him Congo. Congo explains how he would have gouged out his master's eyes, and then other boys break their masters' legs and amputate their arms, and when someone curls his fingers into a claw and twists off his master's balls, everyone cups his crotch in agony before laughing. Enjoy how wonderful it feels to laugh at that moment, and as you walk home, with Doug-lass staring somberly out of your back pocket, wish black history had some funny parts.

Find a funny part. One has been captured on an FBI wiretap of Martin Luther King, Jr., in which he's in a hotel having sex and at the right moment yells, "I'm fuck-ing for God!" The funniness is not immediately appar-ent, though, because you are twenty-five now and King *is* your hero and the woman with whom he is performing God's work is not his wife. Wonder with indignation how he could do such a thing, but come to terms with the com-plexity of humankind and the idea of moral subjectivism while smoking the second of three bongs. Now it is clear that the important thing here is not the messenger but rather the message. It is also clear that the message bears repeating.

After you repeat it, your girlfriend looks confused. She opens her mouth as if to respond but all she does is stare up at you, not even blinking when a bead of sweat falls from your forehead onto hers. Try to explain that you are only quoting some black history but be overtaken by the giggles and conclude that this is a conversation for a different time, when you have not smoked three bongs and are not doing God's work. And maybe it is a conversation for a different person too, because this one is white and does not like to talk about race. She does not even *see* race, she has said, having taught herself to judge individuals solely by their character and deeds. She is post-racial, the first post-racial person you have ever known, but because the term has not yet been invented you just think she's stupid. And because you are the first person she has ever known who has taught himself to see race in everything, she thinks you are stupid too. In time, you both seek and find smarter companions.

Yours, like Frederick Douglass, is, to use a phrase from that earlier era, a mulatto. This appeals to you a great deal because you know mulattos give race a lot of thought, and so this girlfriend probably will not mind helping you see it in places you might have missed. And maybe she can understand it in ways you cannot, since her perspective was shaped not by a stereotypical ghetto experience, like yours, but by a stereotypical suburban experience, like the Fonz's.

"It wasn't quite like his," she says.

The schools she attended were excellent; her neighborhood was safe; the parks and streets were pristine; racial diversity was negligible; the community had its own Fourth of July parade. As you remind her of these facts, sense her getting uptight and diffuse her discomfort with a wide grin and a bad joke, something along the lines of her only run-in with the police being with an officer named Friendly.

She nearly smiles.

Give her two thumbs up at the hip and say, "*Aeyyyyyy!*"

She does smile as she calls you a moron. "But seriously," she continues, and do not interrupt when she relates some of the challenges she faced as one of the few black kids in high school. You have been disappointed by how little she talks about race, to say nothing of her inability to see it everywhere, so her self-pity is a rare treat. Nod sympathetically when she broadens her grievances to include her family; the stares and snickers her parents faced in restaurants; how her brother was routinely followed by mall security; how her sister had trouble getting a date for the prom. Say that while these are excellent blemishes on her community, they are relatively benign. Some people, like you, for instance, lived in communities with drugs, gangs, crime, bad schools, police brutality, and the collective view that white people were and would always be racists. Let the conversation end as she concludes that, should you have children, her stereotype is preferable to yours.

Have children, two boys, two years apart, and decide that neither stereotype will do. The ghetto was never an option but do not be thrilled about raising your sons to be Fonzies. Want a racially diverse, progressive, urban community, but instead move to one that is 96 percent white, conservative, and rural. It is in a college town thirty miles south of Boston, where you and your wife land professorships, the primary appeal being that your house is only a block from campus. It is also, the realtor tells you, on the parade route. Buy four lawn chairs. Sit in one next to your wife and sons on the Fourth of July and wave American flags at the procession. Enjoy this. Your boys are happy.

Later that evening, wrestle with this question: How long will your boys be happy in a 96 percent white, conservative, rural town thirty miles south of Boston?

The answer for your older son, now five, is sixty-eight more days.

That is when you come home from teaching one afternoon and your wife informs you that one of his classmates told him people with his skin color are stinky. Your son reported this incident while crying, but that night he appears to be fine, based on your observations of him, conducted from his bedroom closet. For the twenty minutes you have been in there, he and his little brother have lain in their adjacent beds chatting about cartoon characters and imaginary friends and a new fire truck they wish to own. When they finally fall asleep, sneak out and report the good news to your wife, though caution that more observations will be necessary. In the meantime, you say, that classmate of his should be disciplined. Curl your fingers into a claw and tell your wife you are twisting off his tiny, five-year-old balls.

"First of all," your wife responds, "the person who said it is a girl. Second, let's not make a big deal out of this. I've already told him that she was just being silly. I'm sure he's already forgotten the whole incident."

Dispute this. Tell her that kids remember these sorts of things, sometimes for decades. Tell her about Congo. Imagine Congo's father learning of his son's nickname and later that night hiding in his closet, watching to see if he cries.

A few weeks pass and your son has not cried again. Decrease but do not suspend the observations. Remain on edge, as there are many kids out there who at any moment could say something potentially harmful with long-term consequences.

This is exactly what happens. And this time the culprit is your older son's little brother. He recently started preschool and has noticed that his skin color more closely resembles the other kids' than his brother's, and that his brother's skin color more closely resembles yours than your wife's, and that your wife's skin color is closer in resemblance to his than to his grandmother's, and that his grandmother's skin color is exactly the same as that of the kids in preschool, except for the brown spots on her hands. He turns to his six-year-old brother and asks, "Why is skin different colors?"

A beat passes before your older son responds, "I don't know."

Wonder if this is the moment to have your first important discussion with your sons about race. You can do this by revisiting that "stinky" comment, for starters, and then by warning them of other insults they'll likely receive, though be sure to note that insults, relatively speaking, are not much compared to what they'll learn studying a history that is not very funny. Determine that yes, the time for this talk has come, and then watch it evaporate when your sons scream bloody murder as you emerge—perhaps too quickly—from their closet. Fail at your attempts to calm them before your wife hurries into their room and catches the full rush of their bodies. She sits with them on the bed as they wail through tears that you frightened them. Your wife gives you a look that foretells a coming drought of affection, and your boys give you looks that make you seriously question if you have the capacity to be a good father.

Conclude that you probably do not, but decide to give yourself a fighting chance by ending your subjection to race. Tonight the boys will sleep with their mother, and you will sleep alone in their room, but tomorrow evening, while the boys are in the den playing with their new fire truck, find your wife. She will be sitting at the kitchen table grading papers. Scoop her a dish of mint ice cream. Lower yourself across from her. Stare into her eyes and say this: *You have seen how a man was made a slave; you shall see how a slave was made a man.* She will look confused. Explain.

DRAGON SLAYERS

I was at a Christmas party with a man who wanted me to hate him. I should hate *all* whites, he felt, for what they have done to me. I thought hard about what whites have done to me. I was forty, old enough to have accumulated a few unpleasant racial encounters, but nothing of any lasting significance came to mind. The man was astonished at this response. "How about *slavery*?" he asked. I explained, as politely as I could, that I had not been a slave. "But you *feel* its effects," he snapped. "Racism, discrimination, and prejudice will *always* be a problem for you in this country. White people," he insisted, "are your *oppressors*." I glanced around the room, just as one of my oppressors happened by. She was holding a tray of canapés. She offered me one. I asked the man if, as a form of reparations, I should take two.

It was midway through my third year in academia. I had survived mountains of papers, apathetic students, cantankerous colleagues, boring meetings, sleep deprivation, and two stalkers, and now I was up against a man who had been mysteriously transported from 1962. He even looked the part, with lavish sideburns and solid, black-rimmed glasses. He wasn't an academic, but rather the spouse of one. In fact, he had no job at all, a dual act of defiance, he felt, against a patriarchal and capitalistic society. He was a fun person to talk with, especially if, like me, you enjoyed driving white liberals up the wall. And the surest way to do that, if you were black, was to deny them the chance to pity you.

He'd spotted me thirty minutes earlier while I stood alone at the dining room table, grazing on various appetizers. My wife, Brenda, had drifted off somewhere, and the room buzzed with pockets of conversation and laughter. The man joined me. I accepted his offer of a gin and tonic. We talked local politics for a moment, or rather he talked and I listened, because, being relatively new to this small town, it wasn't something I knew much about, before moving on to the Patriots, our kids, and finally my classes. He was particularly interested in my African American Literature course. "Did you have any black students?" he inquired.

"We started with two," I said, "but ended with twenty-eight." I let his puzzled expression linger until I'd eaten a stuffed mushroom. "Everyone who takes the course has to agree to be black for the duration of the semester."

"Really?" he asked, laughing. "What do they do, smear their faces with burnt cork?"

"Not a bad idea," I said. "But for now, they simply have to think like blacks, but in a way different from what they probably expect." I told him that black literature is often approached as records of oppression, but that my students don't focus on white cruelty but rather its flip side: black courage. "After all," I continued, "slaves and their

immediate descendants were by and large heroic, not
pathetic, or I wouldn't be standing here."

The man was outraged. "You're letting whites off the
hook," he said. "You're absolving them of responsibility, of
the obligation to atone for past and present wrongs . . ."
He went on in this vein for a good while, and I am pleased
to say that I goaded him until he stormed across the room
and stood with his wife, who, after he'd spoken with her,
glanced in my direction to see, no doubt, a traitor to the
black race. That was unfortunate. I'd like to think I betray
whites too.

More precisely it's the belief that blacks are primarily
victims that I betray, a common view held by both races. I,
too, held it for many years. When I was in my early twenties and making my first crude attempts at writing fiction,
I'd sit at my word processor and pound out stories brim-
ming with blacks who understood only anger and pain.
My settings were always ghettos, because that was what
I knew, and the plots centered on hardship and suffer-
ing, because I knew that too. And I also knew this: white
society was responsible for the existence of this miserable
world, and it was my duty as a black artist to make this
clear. Three of these stories gained me acceptance into
the Iowa Writers' Workshop. It was there that my awaken-
ing occurred.

My first course was with Frank Conroy, the program's
director. He was brutally honest and harbored a militant
obsession with clarity. Most of the two-hour-long classes
were spent with him shredding the stories and our egos.
We squirmed in our seats and wiped our brows as he did
his infamous line-by-line, zeroing in on words and phrases
that confused the work's meaning or failed to make
unequivocal sense. It was the most intense and best writ-

ing class that I'd ever had. I went into the second semester confident that my prose had improved and that the most difficult course was behind me.

Randomly, I decided to take a workshop with James Alan McPherson. During the break before classes resumed, I read for the first time his books *Hue and Cry* and *Elbow Room*. The impact his writing had on me was profound. He, too, chronicled the lives of African Americans, and he had done it in short story form, my genre of choice at the time; this was the model I'd been searching for. I read the stories over and over again, convinced that I had found my literary father.

The contrast between Conroy and McPherson could not have been more stark. Conroy was tall, white, and boisterous; McPherson was short, black, and shy. Conroy cursed, yelled, laughed, and joked; McPherson rarely spoke at all, and when he did his voice was so quiet you often could not hear him. The students dominated his workshops. I was disappointed. McPherson was a Pulitzer Prize winner, after all, the first African American to receive that honor for fiction. He was the recipient of a MacArthur "Genius" grant, as well as countless other awards. I wanted his wisdom. I wanted his insight. He gave it mid-semester, when it was time to workshop my first story.

"Before we begin today," he said, "I'd like to make a few comments." This was new; he'd never prefaced a story before. A smile crept on my face as I allowed myself to imagine him praising me for my depiction of a den of heroin addicts, for this was not easy to do, requiring, among other things, an intimate knowledge of heroin addicts and a certain flair for profanity.

"Are you all familiar with gangster rap?" McPherson asked. We were, despite the fact that, besides me, all of the students were white and mostly middle to upper class. While we each nodded our familiarity with the genre, McPherson reached into a shopping bag he'd brought and removed a magazine. He opened it to a premarked page on which was a picture of a rapper, cloaked in jewelry and guns and leaning against the hood of a squad car. Behind him was a sprawling slum. "This person raps about the ghetto," McPherson said, "but he doesn't live in the ghetto. He lives in a wealthy white suburb with his wife and daughter. His daughter attends a predominantly white, private school. That's what this article is about." He closed the magazine and returned it to the bag. "What some gangster rappers are doing is using black stereotypes because white people eat that stuff up. But these images are false, they're dishonest. Some rappers are selling out their race for personal gain." He paused again, this time to hold up my story. "That's what this writer is doing with his work." He sat my story back on the table. "Okay, that's all I have to say. You can discuss it now."

For a few seconds, the only sound in the room was of my labored breathing. And then someone said, "McPherson's right. The story is garbage."

"Complete rubbish," said another.

And so it went from there.

I did not sleep that night. At 8 a.m., when I could hold out no longer, I called McPherson at home and demanded a conference. He agreed to meet me in his office in ten minutes.

He was there when I arrived, sitting behind his desk. The desk was bare except for a copy of my story, and the office was bare except for the desk and two chairs. The built-in bookshelves held nothing, and nothing hung on the walls. There was no dressing on the window, no tele-

phone, and no computer. It might have been the jani-
tor's office, a place to catch a few winks while the mopped
floors dried. And McPherson might have been the jani-
tor. His blue shirt was a mass of wrinkles and his eyes
were bloodshot. His trademark hat, a beige straw Kangol,
seemed to rest at an odd angle on his head; from beneath
it a single long braid had worked its way free and dangled
rebelliously behind his right ear. He noticed me staring at
it and poked it back into concealment.

"Are you okay?" he asked. His voice was gentle, full of
concern. "You sounded like a crazy man on the phone."

"Well, I'm *not* a crazy man." I reached forward to tap
my finger on my story and proceeded to rant and rave as
only a crazy man could. "I did not make this stuff up," I
insisted. "I'm *from* the ghetto." I went through the characters one by one, citing various relatives on whom they
were based, and I mentioned that, just the week before,
my younger brother had been shot in the back while in
McDonald's. I told him I had another brother who was
in and out of prison, a heroin-addict sister-in-law, that
I had once been arrested for car theft (falsely, but that
was beside the point), and that many, many of my friends
were still living in the miserable community in which I
had been raised. "You misread my story," I said in conclusion, "and you misread *me*." I leaned back and folded my
arms across my chest, waiting for his apology. Instead, I
watched as he sprang from his chair and hurried from the
room. He turned left into the hall, and a moment later he
passed going right, with Frank Conroy calling after him,
and then they passed left again, now with Connie Brothers, the program's administrator, in tow, and after two
more passes this awful parade came to an end somewhere
out of view. Now Connie stood before me, looking as nauseous as I felt. "Jim is the kindest soul on Earth," she said
quietly. "Why, why would you insult him?"

For an instant, I saw myself at twelve, looking at a closed front door, behind which was my first love, who had just dumped me and left me standing on her porch trying, unsuccessfully, not to cry.

Connie magically produced a tissue and handed it to me. She rubbed my shoulders while I rambled incoherently, something about sleep deprivation and McPherson being my father. "It's okay, sweetie," Connie said. "I'll talk to him."

McPherson returned momentarily. I apologized. He told me it was okay, that workshops can make people uptight and sensitive. It had been difficult for him too, he explained, when he was a student there in the seventies. There was a lull in the conversation before he asked, "So, where're your people from?"

He still does not believe me, I thought. I mumbled, "Chicago."

"No, no. That's where they *are*. Where are they *from?*"

"Oh, sorry. Arkansas."

"Mine are from Georgia," he said. He smiled and added, "That place is a *motherfucker.*"

The essence of black America was conveyed in that response, a toughness of spirit, humor laced with tragedy, but at that moment all I saw was the man who had rejected my vision. Defeated, I thanked him for agreeing to meet with me as I rose to leave. He stood and shook my hand. As I was walking out the door, he called my name. I turned to face him.

"Stereotypes are valuable," he said. "But *only* if you use them to your advantage. They present your readers with something they'll recognize, and it pulls them into what appears to be familiar territory, a comfort zone. But once they're in, you have to move them beyond the stereotype. You have to show them what's real."

"What's real?" I asked.

Without hesitation, he said, "You."

It was one of those things that you instantly recognize as profound, and then, because you do not quite understand it, try to forget as quickly as you can. It was also one of those things that you cannot forget. And so it roamed freely in my subconscious, occasionally coming into sharp focus to remind me of its presence, but I allowed myself to be consumed by it no more than I would a housefly. For about a year. And then I went to see him again.

"I was wondering," I said, "if you wouldn't mind supervising an independent project."

"That depends," he responded, "on what you'd like to study."

"Me," I said. "I want to study me."

We started with black folklore and history. Next we moved on to blues and jazz, and then we covered a broad range of black literature and culture. We studied black intellectuals and philosophers, sociologists, anthropologists, activists, filmmakers, and ex-cons. For four years, we dissected nearly every aspect of black life and thought, and in the process a theme emerged that had been there all along: *life* is a motherfucker; living it anyway, and sometimes laughing in the process, is where humanity is won.

And this is what I learned about me: I had become my own stereotype, a character in one of my short stories who insisted on seeing himself primarily as a repository of pain and defeat, despite overwhelming evidence to the contrary. The very people with whom I had been raised and had dedicated myself to rendering in prose had become victims of my myopia. My stories showed people being affected by drug addiction, racism, poverty, murder, crime, violence, but they said nothing about the spirit that, despite being confronted with what often amounted to certain defeat, would continue to struggle and aspire for something better. That old slave song "We Shall Overcome" pretty much says it all.

The coursework I conducted with McPherson ultimately contributed to a doctorate in interdisciplinary studies. McPherson served as my dissertation chair. I knew when I started my academic career that I owed him a debt to teach black literature in a certain way. "Less time needs to be spent on the dragons," he told me once, "and more on our ability to forge swords for battle, and the skill with which we've used them."

The man at the Christmas party, of course, would rather that I talk about the dragons. And at first, when students take my class, they are surprised, even a bit disappointed, to see the course will not head in that direction. But by the end of the semester, they are invariably uplifted by the heroic nature of African Americans, in part, perhaps, because it is the nature found in us all. Sometimes students thank me for this approach. On occasion they ask me where I got the idea. I tell them I got it from my father.

BEFORE GRIEF

Before the glove; before the anorexia and addictions; before the moonwalk and crotch grabs and Fred Astaire's admiration and envy; before his color faded and his nose shriveled; before he stunned and confused me, entwining one arm with Brooke Shields's and nestling Emmanuel Lewis with the other; before he was said to be spending some nights with Lisa Marie and other nights alone in an oxygen chamber; before Bubbles and the boa constrictor and the rest of the menagerie that he'd come to trust more than people; before the people he finally *did* trust mentioned "Jesus juice" and sleepovers and gave me reason not to trust *him*, another reason to wonder if now was the time for my disavowal, the moment when I'd say, at last, I've had enough, but I doubted I ever could, because before all of this there was the dazzling child vocalist with a pink gangster hat slicing toward one eye, his four brothers dancing at his side, while the Walker Six—that's what we called ourselves—mimicked their act, imagined that it was us on Ed Sullivan's stage, blowing people's minds.

Though my siblings and I were only having fun, just messing around, for Michael this was serious business, this was *work*—like performing was work for James Brown, the man whose style he had already mastered, like performing was work for Smokey Robinson, the man whose soul he had already cloned. The fact that Michael was less than half their age was part of his appeal, because implicit in his youth was the promise of more, the hope that there'd be years and then decades of watching his legend unfold. But for now it was still 1969, a blustery December evening, bringing to a close a blustery American decade, assassinations and race riots at our heels, and the Walker Six, dumbstruck to see a black family on TV, was bantering over who should sing lead.

My twin brother's case was strong. Like Michael, Jim was the youngest of the group, having departed our mother's womb a full twelve minutes after me. But I owned a pink gangster hat (really a brown skullcap, but still . . .), Mary could reach those high notes, Linda could hold a tune, Tommy was the best dancer, while Timmy, by his own estimation, was the cutest. All of these points were argued compellingly but a little too loudly, prompting our father to threaten corporal punishment, ending a debate that would erupt again the next morning when we heard "I Want You Back" on the living-room console. I don't remember how or if the matter was resolved—perhaps we were *all* Michael—only that the volume was cranked up and we fell into our clumsy choreography, dipping in time to off-key voices, arms open wide as we implored six loves to return.

While we were being Michael, our parents were being his parents—stern, loving, optimistic, highly religious, and always on the lookout for an escape hatch, some elusive portal that would lead us to better opportunities.

They would find that portal in 1970, issuing out into a middle-class enclave on Chicago's South Side. Until then we lived in a ghetto not unlike the Jacksons' in Gary, Indiana, a mere thirty miles away. But that night in 1969, it was clear that their family would be leaving soon, carried off to the good life—not by talent, our parents stressed, but by the values that had seen it to fruition. No loitering in the streets for Michael and his brothers, no slacking in school, no messing around with drugs and gangs, and certainly no being spared the rod, because this was before belts and the backs of hands were considered cruel weapons, before parents' desire to instill discipline and respect in their children, by any means necessary, was considered wrong. "Hard *work*," our father said that night, over the applause of the Ed Sullivan studio audience, "is what got those boys to where they are." To which our mother added, "Hard work *and*, of course, God."

Theirs was named Jehovah. In the eyes of some black folk, that made the Jacksons a little strange. But at least most people had *heard* of the Jehovah's Witnesses, whereas very few had heard of our religion, the Worldwide Church of God, and that made the Walkers even stranger. Like the Jacksons' faith, ours forbade celebrating Christmas, Halloween, birthdays, and Easter, and we were also discouraged from socializing with non-members, resulting in siblings being not just siblings but also best friends. And so I understood that the childhood bond between Michael and his brothers and sisters was both strong and vital, exactly like the bond between my brothers and sisters and me. But this was before the Walker Six grew up and apart, slowly establishing and tending to separate lives, just as the Jackson Five became The Jacksons, and then The Jacksons became Michael, and then Michael became the King.

Now the King is dead. Word of his overdose in 2009 sent the media into a frenzy that weeks later was still going strong. Many people felt this was justified, a sensible response to his unparalleled fame. Others disagreed. "I've seen so many good people the last few days," said one New York politician, "who aren't going to get credit for anything, and then I see this guy, who's really a lowlife, and he's being treated like a hero of civilization." A reporter at the *Washington Post* echoed this theme: "The coverage is out of control, and it's becoming an embarrassment to the news business." Another reporter commented in his blog, "This country has misplaced priorities and a lack of moral values. We celebrate the lives of freaks, yet neglect real heroes." I dismissed these critics and all others too. They didn't understand Michael, I reasoned, but that was before the 2019 documentary *Leaving Neverland* accused him in stark detail of child molestation and rape, and I'd realize I didn't understand him either. But I'd understand this: I *still* couldn't disavow him, at least not fully, because long before a documentary gave me pause a cartoon gave me pride.

The first episode of *The Jackson 5ive* aired in 1971. It was a Saturday, our Sabbath, which meant watching television was forbidden, so the Walker Six was stunned when our parents made an exception. Breaking the Sabbath was a violation of God's law, pretty significant stuff, but then so, too, was an all-Negro cartoon. Something important was happening in the country, our parents understood, a new level of racial tolerance and acceptance, being brought about by a family that looked and behaved like our own. And so my parents sanctioned those Saturday morning viewings, and it was okay for us to spend our allowances on the Jackson Five albums, T-shirts, and posters. It was okay to stay up late after their television specials in 1971 and 1972 to practice our routine. And in 1976, when the Jacksons launched their variety show, the first black family to have one, it was okay to say that Donny and Marie Osmond were lame.

Two years later, the Jacksons were also lame. Michael must have thought so too, because he was already busy on his first solo album, *Off the Wall*, which debuted in 1979, when I was fifteen and seeking, like Michael, my own way. I'd found it by 1982 when *Thriller* was released, and by some bizarre fate it was as if the portal I'd entered this time led me directly to the music video of his title song, a world of ghouls and goblins, otherwise known as pushers and pimps. This was during a terrible period of chaos and wrong choices for me, when the only family I was close to was two of my brothers, who'd climbed through portals similar to mine. While I do not know if this is true, I have a vague memory that the three of us, in 1983, watched the *Motown 25* television special together, and maybe we rose at some point to attempt Michael's moonwalk before collapsing back into our seats, succumbing to the dope coursing through our veins, much as dope would course through Michael's, nearly three decades later, and stop his heart.

Mine stopped, for a moment, when I heard the news. And in that pause before grief, I had a vision of the Walker Six, dancing and singing . . . and then it was gone.

INAUGURATION

Brenda and I watched the inauguration in bad company. Our two Tonkinese cats sat before the window entwined in a beam of sun, wholly disinterested in the promise of a post-racial world, while we sat nearby on the couch, wholly transfixed. Like most other black Americans, we had wanted to attend the event in person; now I regretted that we had not gone. Since my mother lived near D.C., the run on hotels would not have affected us, but we were convinced to stay by other considerations, the main one being our sons. Attempting to endure hours of frigid weather with a six- and eight-year-old would have reduced a festive occasion to a marathon of whines and complaints, to which I would have contributed my share.

We had toyed with the idea of keeping the boys home from school. For weeks I had envisioned them on our laps, eating popcorn and Skittles as I put the inauguration in a meaningful yet delicate context. But pulling that off would have been difficult; I simply had no idea how to express the full weight of the event without offering specific reference to the misdeeds of our nation's past. I did not even know how to talk to them about race. Until very recently I responded to their innocent inquiries regarding the varieties of skin color in purely biological terms; it was not until the morning after Obama's election, in fact, that I attempted to add a social dimension.

At the time, Brenda was in the shower. The boys were in the kitchen, half-asleep and staring incomprehensibly at their bowls of Cheerios. When I walked into the room and told them Obama had won, they shifted their confused gazes to me. "Remember who he is?" I asked.

"The one with the high levels of melanin?" inquired Adrian, my oldest.

"Exactly," I said. "Like us."

Dorian yawned.

I slowly lapped the island, pausing before them with my hands on the back of a chair. "Do you know what the election of Barack Obama means?"

They stared intently at me for a long while. Finally, with great seriousness, Dorian said, "That we can play Mario Cart today after school?"

I realized I was holding my breath. "Sure," I said, exhaling. "Why not?" They cheered. I cheered too, for the conversation had come to a merciful end.

Now, two months later, it was time for me to venture onto that minefield again. But not that morning. Instead of keeping them home from school, I decided it was best for them to experience the inauguration with kids their own age, the generation that, in their adulthood, would mark this occasion the way my generation marked the violent death of American leaders; the way my parents' generation marked the violent death of American wealth.

I should not have thought of death at that moment. After doing so constantly since Obama emerged from the heartland as a legitimate contender and the object of would-be assassins, I felt I had earned the right, on that historic day, to be filled with only positive thoughts. Change for the country, I reasoned, could also mean change for me. I squeezed Brenda's hand, which had been in mine off and on for the last hour. She squeezed back. We shared a quick smile before I placed my feet on the coffee table, burrowed deeper in the sofa, and gave in to this unfolding social experiment.

During the next ninety minutes we were treated to the wisdom of pundits, musical performances, and a number of interviews with ecstatic members of the swelling crowd. At regular intervals fleets of school buses arrived, out of which tumbled children carrying hand-made Obama signs, and each time I was reminded of my sons. In a short while they would become racially conscious, made aware that the seemingly blank page of skin pigmentation was actually filled with script. I assumed their teachers would offer context for the inauguration as I would have, taking care not to have the black students feel singled out or unduly uncomfortable, sensitive to the fact that so few of them attended their private school.

And yet no matter how carefully delivered, words are still words, and I feared their impact. *Class, before you watch the inauguration, there's something you should know. Black people were brought to this land in chains because it was widely believed by whites that they were inferior. But President Lincoln knew all humans were equal, and that's why, after two hundred and fifty years of captivity, he declared the slaves free.* Context provided, the teachers would march their classes into the all-purpose room to watch the unforeseeable fruits of Lincoln's decree. Maybe my sons would move just a step slower than the others. And maybe no one would notice. Not even my sons. But the seed of self-doubt would have been planted, and over time it would manifest itself as sullenness, a lack of desire to compete that appears so often in African American males, even those of privilege . . . or it would have no impact on them at all, serving simply as another example of man's inhumanity to man that can be found the world over, through all of time. Context is everything.

This was the context for me: I was forty-five, the son of a teacher, the grandson of sharecroppers, the great-grandson of slaves. The lower branches of my ancestral tree bore the weight of the lynched; the higher branches bore the weight of the embittered. Such was the landscape of the ghettos in which I had been raised, where many of the adults I knew hated whites, believed racism was insurmountable, and felt obliged to offer their children this bleak worldview. The mere mention of the phrase "post-racial" was inconceivable. But then, the election of a black president was too.

The inauguration had ended and Brenda was back on campus, fulfilling her academic duties. I did not teach on Tuesdays, so I remained at home, fulfilling my duties as dad. I had helped Dorian and Adrian with their homework, overseen piano practice, denied several requests to watch television, and joined them in a few games of Mario Cart. That was the easy part. In a few minutes I would walk upstairs to where they were playing in their room to discuss Obama's presidency. This decision was motivated less by a desire to dispense knowledge than to receive it. I was anxious to know what their teachers had said to them and how, or if, they had responded.

Their faces had yielded nothing. Nor had their moods. Their school had a "drive-through" pick-up system, whereby parents and caretakers pulled up near the entrance and children were escorted out to the idling cars. As Adrian and Dorian had approached mine two hours ago, I had studied their faces, looking for *what?*— I didn't know—and yet hoping I would not find it. I did not. They were their typical public selves, quiet and reserved, until we had pulled away from the building, at which point they burst into animated conversation, as if duct tape had been suddenly ripped from their mouths. But the topics they covered did not include the inauguration, and I had not psyched myself up enough to mention it until now.

As I climbed the stairs, I was reminded of my twin brother and I being thirteen and having our first serious talk with our father. We had been summoned to the living room, where we found him sitting on the edge of the couch, looking grave. "Boys," he said, rising, "you're old enough to start being with girls, but if you're going to be out there *tomcat'n*, you'll need these." He held up a hand, in which were several sex education brochures. "When you're ready for them," he continued, "they'll be on top of the refrigerator." And then he left. This was not the model I intended to follow when it came time to broach the subject of sex with Dorian and Adrian. But at that moment, as I entered their room to broach the subject of race, I wished there was something that, right before leaving, I could hold up and say, *Boys, you're old enough to start being black, but if you're going to be out there Negro'n, you'll need these.*

"Hi, Daddy," they said in synch.

They were sitting on the floor, amidst a herd of stuffed animals. I joined them. "Hi, boys. What are you doing?"

"Playing with our friends," Dorian said. "You can play too." He handed me a giraffe as he explained the rules, which required the person holding the giraffe to be mugged. A full-scale wrestling match ensued, our favorite activity since they learned to walk. They had tripled in size since then, but I had tripled my determination to remain fit for battle. I ran on the treadmill each day; I lifted weights five times a week; I counted my caloric intake the way a miser counts his money. And yet a mere ten minutes into the match I was winded.

Ignoring their protests, I called a time-out. Now the three of us lay on the floor, staring at the ceiling as if at interesting cloud formations. It *was* interesting, I supposed, that the surface had dipped a full six inches in the center and that the middle seam was starting to peel—telltale signs that the plaster had loosened from the support beams. This had happened in the dining room a year earlier, resulting in a $2,000 repair and a reiteration of my vow to never again buy a house described as "antique."

"Are you ready?" asked Adrian.

"Not yet," I replied.

"How much longer?" This was from Dorian.

"Not much," I said. I'd caught my breath but I was stalling.

"Now?" Dorian asked a moment later.

"Almost," I said. "First I want to talk to you about the inauguration. Did you see it at school today?"

"Yes," they responded.

"What did you think?"

"It was good," offered Adrian.

"It was long," Dorian noted.

We were quiet for a second. "Did your teachers explain why it was so important?"

"Because Barack Obama is the first black president," Adrian said.

I turned toward him. "And?"

"And what?"

"Is that all she said?"

"Yes."

I faced Dorian. "Did your teacher tell you that too?"

He nodded.

"Nothing more?"

He shook his head. "Can we wrestle now?"

"In a moment." I sat my giraffe on the floor. Then I looked back at the ceiling and spoke about slavery, offering a broad overview of what I knew they would soon cover in school. When I finished I watched Adrian as he picked up one of the stuffed animals, a large penguin, and waddled it across the air. Dorian was galloping a pony on his belly. They did not seem particularly interested in what I had said, but, like my father's sex education brochures, the information had been made available for future use. And that was why I gave them this too: "To go from slavery to the presidency means that African Americans are remarkable people, capable of achieving anything."

"Like becoming an artist," Dorian stated matter-of-factly.

"Of course, if that's what you want."

Dorian nodded.

Adrian said, "Me too. Dorian and I are going to be artists together. We'll have our own studio."

"And," Dorian added, "it'll be painted red and blue. Red is my favorite color. Blue is Adrian's."

Faced with the decision to reel the conversation back in or to let it float away, I chose the latter. I imagined it as a helium-filled balloon, pushing through the failing seam of our ceiling-cloud and into the stratosphere. And that, it occurred to me, was as it should be.

I reached for the giraffe. The boys instantly pounced on me—so, too, did a sense of optimism similar to what I had felt at the conclusion of Obama's speech. It had been characteristically upbeat, designed to appeal to our better nature, including the nature, it seemed, of the Tonkinese. Both cats had joined Brenda and me by then, one on each lap, their bellies offered up for gentle strokes. We obliged, and soon their purrs mingled with the cheers of the crowd, and our sniffles.

KALESHION

Kaleshion isn't a word in the dictionary. It's a word on your barber's wall, handwritten beneath a photo of a bald head. There are other photos of heads up there with made-up words to identify their haircuts, but your father never selects those because they require hair. Male preschoolers with hair, your father believes, is a crime to which he'll no more be party to than genocide. Your friends' fathers feel similarly, so your friends are bald too. But when they turn seven or eight and certainly by nine their fathers let them try different styles, while yours keeps making you get a kaleshion. He makes you get one until you are ten. What's the deal with that? You don't know. All you know is he relaxes his stance in the nick of time because it's 1974 now and the Afro is king. Grow yours the size of a basketball. Swear on your grandmother's grave that the kaleshion is behind you forever.

It's never a good idea, unfortunately, to swear on your grandmother's grave. One summer day, for instance, when you are twenty-six and have just moved to a new neighborhood, try out the barbershop near your apartment. It's 1990 and the Afro long since gave way to the Jheri Curl, which gave way to flat tops, which you are not particularly fond of so you wear your hair an inch long all around. As you sit in the chair tell the barber you'd like a trim. Close your eyes. Relax. Nod off after a while but be startled awake when for some reason the clippers graze your upper lip. Ask the barber, "What are you doing?" and when he says, "Tightening up your mustache," respond, "Don't touch my mustache," but he says, "It's too late." Then he says, "I'll just finish this up," as you wonder, "What's this guy's deal?" and his deal is he's incompetent, though you don't know to what extent because the mirror is behind you. But when he spins the chair around you are surprised to discover the mirror is actually a window, through which you see a man in a barber's chair staring back at you, and yet, somehow, the barber standing behind this man's chair is also standing behind yours, which means, in all likelihood, this man is you. It's amazing the difference a kaleshion can make.

"So," the barber asks, "what do you think?" and you think to punch him but instead refuse to pay. He orders you to leave and bans you from returning, which is a misuse of the word *ban*. You can't be banned from doing something you'd never do. That'd be the same as you being banned from eating frog legs or skydiving or from still wearing a Jheri Curl like the guy at work you are about to dethrone as the office laughing stock, though maybe, it occurs to you as you walk home, you can mitigate this fate by shaving off your new pencil mustache. Start to jog with this thought in mind though you would have done well to walk because it's sweltering outside and you haven't jogged in a while. Cut through an alley to shorten the distance, but even with that you arrive on the back porch of your third-floor apartment breathless and sweaty, much like, one could imagine, a drug addict about to commit a burglary.

Your girlfriend imagines this. After parting the curtains she screams and ducks away from the window. Shout her name as you pat your pockets for the keys that are on the kitchen table, then realize she can't hear you because she's in the front room, where the phone is, calling the police. Don't panic; all you'll have to do is tell them about the incompetent barber. Take out your driver's license in order to illustrate that your new face is also your old face. If at least one of the officers is black he'll see the resemblance, but the white one, like your white girlfriend, whose fingers have just parted the curtains again, will give you the stink eye. There is a high likelihood both officers will be white, however, which means weapons could come into play, so either convince your girlfriend you are her boyfriend or run. Lift your driver's license to the window. Press it against the glass. Watch your girlfriend squint at your photo, then at you, and then again at your photo. Beg her to let you in. A voice in your head orders you to get the hell out of there just as something in hers clicks; one hand cups her mouth, the other releases the curtain. The deadbolt and your fate turn.

Moments later, while shaving off your mustache, vow to never set foot in another barbershop. This doesn't improve your mood so try another approach at your favorite bar. You feel better during your third cocktail, enough, even, for you to tell the bartender what happened. He doesn't believe you. Lift your baseball cap. When he bursts into laughter you can't help but join him. It *is* funny, after all. Repeat the part about seeing the stranger through the window and laugh some more. And when the bartender, who knows you're an aspiring writer, says this would make a good story, smile and say you definitely intend to write it someday.

Write a lot of other stories first, though, which earns you publications, a faculty position, your first book contract and, after many years, an invitation to read at a prestigious literary conference. According to the invitation, there are some notable writers scheduled to participate, one of whom is quite famous. This is a big deal. This is huge! It could mark your arrival as a serious man of letters, and it's too bad, in a way, that your girlfriend isn't around to see it. She was supportive of your early efforts, even serving as your copy editor, an arrangement you'd projected far into a future where you'd discuss comma splices in your hospice, though perhaps you should have taken her attempt to have you arrested as a bad omen. That happened fifteen years ago, a few months before you broke up. A lot has changed since then. One thing that hasn't changed, though, is your self-imposed barbershop ban.

This is the correct use of the word *ban* because, who knows, maybe one day you'll lift it after growing tired of the split-ends and generally scraggly appearance that results from you cutting your own hair. And you might have to start taking your sons to a barbershop when they realize that their hair, which you've cut since they were babies, doesn't have to look like this either. But at ages six and eight they're still too young to pay attention to such things, and you're still wary of barbers, so every couple of weeks you break out the clippers.

Each of you gets the same style, a conservative quarter-inch cut that speaks of sophistication and a desire not to scare white people. You call it The Obama. To achieve it, simply use the #1 clipper guard on the top and the #1/2 for the sides and back. Sometimes you tease your sons by saying you can't find the clipper guards so they'll have to get kaleshions, and when they jump from the chair and run you chase them around the house, all of you laughing wildly. It's a good time. You did this for a while this morning but now, after they've received their Obamas, it's time to give yourself yours. Make this your best effort. The literary conference is tomorrow.

Start on the crown of your head and work your way forward, as you always do, but this time scream because the #1 guard has just tumbled before your face and landed in the sink, followed by a clump of hair. Lean towards the mirror to stare at your long strip of pale scalp. Whisper, "Please God, no, please," but God cannot help you. Nor can your wife, who runs to the bathroom and, much like your girlfriend all those years ago, stares at you with a hand cupping her mouth. Your sons burst into the room. They want to know what the screaming is about. Your wife, speaking into her palm, says, "Daddy's giving himself a kaleshion."

The boys want to see. Reluctantly bend towards them. They erupt in laughter, as if, you imagine, you have just stepped to the podium to give your reading. Shoo them away. Try to convince yourself it's not as bad as you think but the truth of the matter is conveyed by your wife's stink eye. She lowers her hand and asks, "What happened?"

That's simple: the grandmother on whose grave you swore all those years ago reached from the heavens to flick off the clipper guard. But don't say this. Say you're not sure. You are sure, however, of what must be done. Ask your wife for the shoe polish.

"You can't," she responds, "wear shoe polish on your head."

"Why not?"

"Because that's insane."

"You have a better idea?"

"Yes. Shave the rest of your head."

Look horrified and say, "Are you *crazy*?"

"You have to," she insists.

Remind her that the important literary conference is tomorrow.

"Exactly," she responds, and a stalemate is reached.

Twenty-four hours later, arrive at the important literary conference. As you enter the auditorium, a writer you know strikes up a conversation, thereby establishing the expectation that you will sit together, which is fine, as long as he doesn't go to the first row, which he does. Now, thanks to the stadium seating, everyone will have a clear view of the top of your head. But it will not be a view of shoe polish because your wife convinced you not to use it on the grounds it would be difficult to remove. The same effect, she explained, could be achieved with mascara. You don't know much about mascara, having never worn it before, though you are pretty certain that under certain conditions, such as high humidity, it runs. The auditorium feels like a rain forest. You're already sweating. You're already imagining your rectangle of scalp being slowly revealed. You can all but hear the snorts and giggles . . .

Stop obsessing. Distract yourself by perusing the conference's brochure. The first scheduled reader is the famous writer. You saw him when you entered the auditorium, sitting dead center of the room with a few of his books on the desk before him, colorful Post-its sticking from the pages, and a chill went down your spine. Everyone is eager to hear him, no doubt, but allow yourself to believe he's eager to hear you. Why not? Maybe it's true. Maybe he's as much of an admirer of your work as you are of his. You're not famous by a long stretch, but you are, you've noticed, last on the schedule, a position, like first, often reserved for a writer of a certain ability, a certain gravitas.

Gravitas indeed! The famous writer brings down the house and leaves the podium to thundering applause. The next reader is outstanding too. As is the next. Everyone is quite good, although, admittedly, it's difficult to pay close attention while imagining mascara working its way down your head.

Finally, you're introduced. Go to the podium. Look around the room, really for the first time, and take in the size of the crowd. It's enormous! Of the hundred or so seats, only a few are empty, one of which, you note, is the famous writer's. His books are gone too. As indignation bubbles up from some dark place inside you, wonder what's this guy's deal, but the real question, you've already begun to suspect, is what's the deal with you. For a split second you are back in the barber's chair staring into a mirror at a man you don't recognize, a man, this time, who's at an important literary conference with mascara running on his head hoping to impress a famous writer who's ducked out of the room, failing to find this funny. It's amazing the difference an ego can make.

Look away from the famous writer's chair. Greet the audience. Announce that, before you begin, you'd like to take a brief moment, if you could, to talk about your hair. Raise your hands to the heavens. Smile. Now swear, as your beloved grandmother is your witness, that the story you are about to tell is true.

THE HERITAGE ROOM

The Heritage Room was named in honor of its two dozen mounted portraits of famous African Americans. The usual troika of black iconography was there—former slaves, civil rights leaders, and athletes—and each person seemed, if not angry, then intensely displeased. Even Rosa Parks looked like she could kill. For once I'd like to see portraits of famous African Americans smiling or frozen in laughter, their heads tossed back and hands clutching guts as they considered the absurdities and ironies of their lives. That, in fact, was my exact response when I received the sexual harassment complaint filed against me by Judy, the woman sitting far to my left.

In contrast to the sternness of the black portraits, my white colleagues were jovial and lively, bantering with each other about being back on the front lines of education after summers spent traveling and undertaking home improvements. The chair arrived with a plate of cookies, and as the last few were consumed we began the first of the semester's monthly department meetings. This was my eighteenth such meeting, but I still vividly remembered the first; there were twenty-two people in the room, as there were now, and I scanned their faces, trying but unable to recall the names they told me during my interview. The chair remedied that by reintroducing everyone, yet by the time the three-hour meeting adjourned, I had forgotten their names again. But I remembered their types: the Intellectuals, the Comedians, the Socialites, the Rebels, the Complainers, the Mutes. And I, as the English department's first African American hire in its 161-year history, was the Token Negro.

Two years later, after a contentious committee meeting, Judy decided Angry Black Man was a better fit. "As he spoke," she wrote to the department chair, "his face flushed. His hands, which were on the tabletop, formed into fists, and he leaned forward over the table toward other members of the committee." I had done no such thing. Rather, I had merely argued my point during a debate. I tried explaining this to the chair, but to no avail. I was banned from that particular committee for a year. It was during my banishment that, one winter night, I had the occasion of visiting Judy in her office.

It was late, perhaps nine or ten. I often went to campus during this time after Adrian and Dorian were asleep, primarily to clear my head but also to get a little work done. And I often encountered Judy. Middle-aged and single, it may have been the solitude I sought that she was trying to avoid, though no one besides us ever seemed to be in our dark, three-story building. Passing her office, I'd see the profile of her tall, thin form folded behind her desk, the jacket of one of her signature two-piece suits draped over the back of the chair. Without stopping I would say hello, and then later when I was leaving, if she were still there, I would wish her goodnight. She'd respond in kind. No other words would be exchanged. On this night, however, as I passed her office to go home, she called my name.

I returned and stood in her doorway. "So," she asked, smiling broadly as she removed her glasses, "how are things?" Before I could respond, she offered me a seat, motioning towards a chair in front of her desk. It was covered with papers. "Oh, you can put those anywhere," she said. When I hesitated, she added, with a touch of sadness in her voice, "Unless you're in a hurry." I looked at my watch to signal that my time was limited, though this was not the case. I just had a bad feeling about being there.

"I have a few minutes." I moved the papers and eased onto the chair. She inquired about my sons, to begin with, and then she mentioned her nephew, who wanted a certain toy for Christmas that she could not find. Next we talked about some of the highs of the previous year, and then, when we mentioned the lows, I could not help but express my disappointment at being removed from the committee simply because our positions differed.

"I had nothing to do with that," she said.

"I was told you did."

"Well, I'm afraid whoever told you that is mistaken."

"So, you didn't report me to the chair?"

"I don't know that I would use the word *report*. Now, I did mention that I found your behavior unsettling."

"Unsettling?"

"Oh, yes," she said, her hand rising to scratch the base of her neck. "You were so angry it frightened me. I thought you were going to be violent."

I snickered, thinking that there was a time in my life when I would have wanted her to feel this way. In my teens, I had worn my hair in a perm, a la James Brown, weighted my pinkie fingers with bulky costume jewelry, carried a straight razor in my sock, cupped my crotch at every opportunity, and snarled a great deal. I was very frightening. I was also very unoriginal; *every* teenaged male in my neighborhood, it seemed, affected the same countenance. For some, this was the only image that would ever make sense, and they would actively pursue the accompanying roles for which there were no good ends. For others, such as myself, who were both imaginative and cowardly, there would be better roles to play. But for all of us, there had been that centuries-old stereotype of the angry and violent black male that had duped us into thinking that was what we were supposed to be. And it had duped Judy too.

"You realize," I said, "that you are a racist." For a second she looked stricken, as only white liberals can when confronted with such a charge. I understand that it's because, on some level, they know that it is true. Racism is part and parcel of our culture, the great American disease with which we all are afflicted; there will be no cure until we accept this diagnosis. "The only thing I did in that meeting," I continued, "was argue my point. Aggressively, passionately, maybe even self-righteously, but not angrily. And even if I *had* been angry," I added, "black males have a right to that emotion without it being assumed that we are violent."

Her mouth closed momentarily before she stuttered a response, conceding that she might have been mistaken. She apologized. I thanked her, glanced at my watch again, and then rose. She rose too. As I was about to leave, she asked for a hug, absolution, I knew, for her sins. "I'm not a racist," she said quietly as we embraced.

"Of course you are."

She pulled away.

"I'm one too," I continued. "We all are. It's important that this be acknowledged."

She insisted that she had nothing to acknowledge. As if to prove it, at the start of the semester she lobbied for my reinstatement to the committee from which I had been removed.

In the weeks that followed, I continued to encounter her in the building at night, and she continued to invite me into her office. We'd talk for long periods, usually about my boys or her nephew, our classes, occasionally about our colleagues, and once or twice even about race. I began to enjoy our meetings and found myself looking forward to them. She seemed to as well.

But that changed mid-semester. We were again having a committee meeting, and, like before, found ourselves at opposing ends of an issue. As is typical in academia, we argued in circles for a long period and nothing got resolved, but that was not what bothered me. What bothered me was what I saw as her condescension, the fact that she attempted to lecture me on my area of expertise, as if I really were the Token Negro. By the time the meeting ended, I *was* angry and I'm sure it showed; had I sat for a portrait at that moment, it would have fit very nicely with the others in the Heritage Room. And that is the fallacy of those images, for in those same communities where black boys snarl and clutch their crotches, anger is often a prelude to a joke, as there is broad understanding that the triumph over this destructive emotion lay in finding its punch line. Rosa Parks, I am willing to wager, laughed more than she frowned.

I was laughing, in fact, the day after my meeting with Judy and the committee, when I sat at my computer. *Dear Judy,* I wrote, *I hope that you are not fearful that I will physically assault you, as you told me you were before when our opinions differed. When you see me approaching, just remind yourself that I am a college professor, not a hoodlum, and you'll be fine.*

A few days after I sent it, she filed the complaint. She claimed I had sent the email primarily because she was female, and she vehemently denied ever fearing me before now. The six-page condemnation was hysterical and wide-ranging, so convoluted at times that it failed to make sense, and at times so self-incriminating that I was embarrassed for her. The mere assertion that she found my email to be a threat of physical danger showed the extent to which racial stereotypes had invaded her subconscious. I felt bad for her. I regretted sending the email. And I tried not to be too amused by the fact that, in the end, it was her anger, not mine, that was out of control.

The administration agreed. The complaint was dismissed.

Since then I had tried to put the matter behind me, but I still sensed tension from some of my colleagues. And Judy did not speak to me at all. When we approached each other in the corridor, she walked right by, and when I went to our office building at night, she was not there. The only time we were in each other's company for any extended period was in the Heritage Room, where, unlike the portraits surrounding us, I smiled.

UNPREPARED

We drove cautiously through the downpour, making the kind of small talk one would expect of strangers, when my companion slid a jacket from his lap, exposing his penis. It rose up high through his zipper, like a single meerkat surveying the land for trouble. To be sure, there was trouble to be had because, despite being a skinny seventeen-year-old, I never left home without my razor.

But what I'd really needed that morning was an umbrella. Rain had begun falling in sheets a few minutes earlier as I sprinted to catch the Seventy-ninth Street bus, which pulled away just before I reached it. My frustration had not had a chance to sink in when an Oldsmobile stopped in front of me. The driver offered me a ride. I was immediately put on guard, since random acts of kindness were rare for the South Side of Chicago. In the instant before I opened the passenger door, I decided that a robbery would put me back only six dollars, making it worth the risk. But if he had designs on my leather Converse All

Stars, as had a previous robber, I might have to offer some resistance, depending on whether or not he drew a gun.

The other robber had not. He'd merely dragged me into an alley and begun punching my face while explaining, "*This is a stickup, motherfucker!*" Next he searched my pockets, finding and taking my only dollar and a bus transfer. He cursed and hit me once more. Then he jabbed a finger at my shoes. "Give me those!" he commanded. "Give me your coat too!" He didn't seem to mind that it was winter and the ground was covered in snow. After he fled with my belongings, I went back to where he had accosted me to wait for the bus that would complete the final leg of my trip to basketball practice, due to start in about twenty minutes at 7 a.m. When the bus arrived, I explained to the driver what had happened. He waived the fare, gave me a tissue to wipe my bloodied nose, and a few miles later deposited me between stops, right at the fieldhouse door. This had happened five years earlier, when I was only a child of twelve. And unarmed.

"So, do you play sports?" this driver was asking me. He wore a large Afro and lush sideburns that fell to his chin, typical of the current style. I figured him to be around fifty.

"Little bit," I said.

"What do you play?"

"Hoops."

"Oh, yeah?"

I nodded. "Yeah."

"What position?"

"Point guard."

"Going to shoot some now?"

I shook my head. "Work."

"What do you do?"

"I'm a lab assistant at the medical center."

"What does a lab assistant do?"

"Clean piss and shit from test tubes."

"Does that pay well?"

I looked at him. "Well enough."

We stopped at a red light. The wipers slapped at the rain, filling the silence. The penis continued its watch. I looked around myself, amazed at how dark it was for mid-morning, and at how many people, like me, had been caught unprepared. They darted about beneath newspapers or stood huddled in doorways, while I sat relatively dry, convinced that both my six dollars and my All Stars were safe. It was my body this man wanted, and that, I believed, was safe too. When the subject of sex was broached—verbally, that is—I would simply state that men weren't my thing. I relaxed in my seat and waited for his proposition, hoping it wouldn't come before we'd traveled the remaining ten blocks to the elevated train station, where he'd agreed to take me.

Meanwhile, fifteen hundred miles away in Atlanta, another black male may also have believed his body was safe, just prior to being slain and dumped in the Chatta-hoochee River.

His name was Nathaniel Cater. His murder was unusual only in the fact that he was twenty-seven, much older than the other victims, and in the fact that there had been other victims. Twenty by that point, all of them between the ages of nine and fourteen, and all of them black males. The first murder had occurred two years prior, in 1979—a fourteen-year-old boy found in the woods, a gunshot to his head. Nearby was the boy's friend, who had been asphyxiated. A few months later, a ten-year-old boy was found dead in a dumpster. And then a strangled nine-year-old; a stabbed fourteen-year-old; a strangled thirteen-year-old, murder after murder until the capriciousness of Negroes could no longer be sustained as a viable cause. There was clearly a holocaust in the making, a systemic denial of future black generations, a conclusion that flowed logically from the vicious legacy of the Deep South. This was the work of the Ku Klux Klan, people believed, and I believed it too. The South, as promised, was rising again.

Each night, on the evening news, I watched efforts to keep it down. New York's Guardian Angels, the Reverend Jesse Jackson, and grieving parents gave press conferences. There were images of helicopters flying over homes and of bloodhounds sniffing through parks. Psychics traveled through time and returned with tips and warnings. Confidential hotlines collected the names of would-be killers. Rewards were posted. Sammy Davis, Jr. and Frank Sinatra gave a benefit concert. Green ribbons were worn. And through it all, the murders continued to mount, until June 21, 1981—just a month after I'd accepted the ride with the stranger—when the police arrested a twenty-three-year-old man named Wayne Williams.

Being male, single, introverted, and a loner, Williams fit the general profile of a serial killer, except for the all-important fact that he was black. And so rather than a collective sigh of relief in the black community, there was broad outrage, for we all understood that we were *not* serial killers. The arrest of Williams was a smokescreen, it was decided, another cover-up by white supremacists of their sordid deeds. Sure, we had some rotten apples among us, your garden variety of thugs, burglars, prostitutes, gangbangers, and dope dealers. We even had middle-aged men in cars who'd solicit sex from teenaged boys, but the torturing and execution of people for sport or at the behest of inner voices, that *pathological shit,* was the strict domain of white folks. It wasn't in our DNA.

That's why we had not produced an Ed Gein, for instance, the man whose barbarity inspired the movies *Psycho* and *Silence of the Lambs.* When his ten-year killing spree ended, it was discovered that he lived, literally, in a house of horrors, with the flesh of his victims serving as furniture upholstery, jewelry, and clothing. A heart was simmering on the stove. John Wayne Gacy was another; he killed thirty-three boys and men, cutting their throats while in the act of raping them. And how about Herman Mudgett, the doctor who was said to have murdered over two hundred women by asphyxiating them in a secret chamber in his office? Then there was Albert Fish, who may have mutilated and killed up to one hundred boys; Ted Bundy, the necrophiliac who applied makeup to his victims and slept with them until they decomposed; David "Son of Sam" Berkowitz, who killed women by order of a howling dog. The list also includes Richard Angelo, Jeffrey Dahmer, Gary Ridgway, Andrew Cunanan, but no one knew of them yet, because it was still only the spring of 1981, a month before Wayne Williams' arrest and a year before his conviction of the Atlanta Child Murders. All during the trial he maintained his innocence, and I, convinced not of a lack of evidence—there was plenty— but only of our genetic superiority, was among the many blacks who believed him.

By 2019, the fortieth anniversary of those crimes, Williams had yet to own his guilt. But I had long since owned mine. My belief that blacks could be only so bad was equivalent to the view, promulgated since slavery, that we could be only so good; to hold one of these views necessitates the holding of the other. And both views, albeit used for different purposes, place false restrictions on our humanity. At the time of Williams' conviction, I was incapable of reaching this conclusion. The seed of it was planted, however, only three weeks later, when a thirty-three-year-old black man from Michigan, "Coral" Eugene Watts, confessed to killing forty women and girls. His preferred *modi operandi* were death by drowning, strangling, and stabbing, and his preferred race was white. This was in part why he was so difficult to capture, since a defining trait of serial killers is that they rarely kill outside of their own ethnic group, and this was the same trait that, ironically, made the case stronger against Williams. But just as many blacks came to Williams's defense, the impulse was to defend Watts as well, for here might be a vigilante of sorts, an intensely angry brother out to exact the ultimate revenge on his oppressor. That argument couldn't hold water, though; all it took was for Watts to explain that he'd dreamed of killing women since he was twelve, describe at length his conversations with demons, and express his need to drown some of his victims in order to keep their evil spirits from floating free. This was no vigilante. This was just a man—as vile and deranged as any white counterpart who had preceded him or who would follow. And he, like Wayne Williams, and like Gein, Bundy, Mudgett and the others, belonged to us all.

As did my driver. As did I. And so the scenario in which we found ourselves that rainy morning was susceptible to the full range of human behavior, not merely the one I had envisioned and, luckily, the one that played out. A block from my destination, he removed a twenty-dollar bill from his shirt pocket and positioned it on the seat between us. Just before that we'd spoken of the Bulls, the White Sox, the storm, and then, as the train station came into view, he circled the conversation back to my job cleaning test tubes at the medical center. "I wouldn't care for that," he said. "Do you like it?"

"It's just a job," I said. "Pays the bills."

It was the wrong thing to say, or maybe it was the right thing, because my reference to money brought the issue to the fore. It was then that he'd presented the twenty-dollar bill. "Would you like to make a little extra?" he asked, winking at me. "Have a little fun in the process?"

I stated the response I'd mentally rehearsed since he'd exposed himself: "Sorry, brother, but men just aren't my thing."

"I can give you forty," he said quickly, as if he'd been mentally rehearsing too. I told him no again. He swore. But I didn't panic. I didn't reach for my razor. I repeated my position and thanked him for the ride. We drove the rest of the way in silence. Just before he stopped the car, he pulled his jacket back onto his lap, picked up the money, and in this manner—without theft, without violence, without murder, without the slightest decrease in my stupidity—the trip came to an end.

FEEDING PIGEONS

My creative writing students are free to choose their own essay topics, and more and more, I've noticed, they involve aspects of being LGBTQ. Some use the occasion to come out, sharing with the class their first baby steps of pride, while others describe the difficulties they've experienced after doing so. Often there are gushing tributes to boyfriends or girlfriends, though I receive a fair amount of breakup narratives too. Once, many years ago, when being a member of this community was much less socially acceptable, a young man wrote a scathing condemnation of homosexuality and same-sex marriage. I kept him after class and failed him for the course.

When I reached my office an hour later, there were three messages from his father. "This is Sal Calvino," the first one began. "Please call me." The next was: "Look, Professor. I don't know what you're trying to pull, but I don't like it." And the third said, "I know what your problem is. You like gays." His son was a plagiarist. I had paid $30 for the proof, courtesy of Essay.com. I called Mr. Calvino and told him this. He stuck to his opinion. "You got a thing for them gays," he said, "don't you?"

I considered his question, my thoughts taking me back nearly three decades to when I was a lab assistant and had become friends with Dr. Jones, a black oncologist who expressed himself with a certain effeminate flair. One day I introduced him to my twin brother, Jim, who had recently been hired as an orderly. They shook hands, and after Dr. Jones excused himself to do his rounds, my brother snickered and asked, "So when did you start hanging out with a *gump*?" I had not heard that expression for many years, not since we were teens. It was frequently used as a form of playful insult, but rarely as a serious accusation. Blacks had had their fill of emasculation over nearly three centuries of slavery; the need to not see male homosexuality in our community was strong. So we did not see our friend Paul's skintight jeans, or the way he tossed his hips while dancing, and the lock of hair he twisted and let dangle before his brow was not there. We saw the tattoo he carved into his arm with a knife dipped in ink. We saw his girlfriends. We saw a man. He still lives in our old neighborhood, his body now ravaged and shriveled, someone recently told me, wrecked by three decades of heroin and booze. But I suspect the lie he leads is the true source of his demise.

The only two openly gay people I knew in my youth were female. One was a gangbanger with lots of scars and muscles. When I was fourteen she beat me up and stole my new shoes, and two years later, when I at last got a steady girlfriend, she stole that too. I was crushed when Crystal told me, because I was in love, but otherwise her revelation caused me no concern. Nothing between us would change, I knew, except the awful fact that I would be single again. We continued to spend a great deal of time together, and she continued to sneak to my house for sleepovers. We would lie on my bed fully dressed, as we had before she was a lesbian, talking for hours and finally falling asleep to the sound of my nine-inch black-and-white TV. One night, she leaned over and asked, "How come you never tried to do it with me?"

I pushed myself up on my elbows. The light from *The Johnny Carson Show* bounced off her face. "I *did* do it with you."

"Once," she said. "But we were drunk, so that didn't count."

"Trust me," I said, "it counted."

"Still, what about all the other chances you had?"

I could not recall any other chances. We had logged hundreds of kissing hours but she had insisted on no more. "You're right," I said. "I could have raped you a half-dozen times, easily."

"Unless . . ."

"Unless?"

"Unless . . . *you're gay too!*" The notion thrilled her. She broke into a smile as she rolled over to hug me. "We could get an apartment together!" she exclaimed. "There's this *cool* gay neighborhood on the North Side called Lakeview. That's where I'm moving next year, as soon as I finish school."

And she did. I did too, but it took me five years, when a new girlfriend landed me there. My apartment was small but in a prime location; a short walk to the beach, near preppy restaurants and bars, and just a mile from a theater specializing in noir films. It was also, as Crystal had said, a gay haven. At all times of day and night, same-sex couples walked openly hand-in-hand, and it was common to see them kissing beneath the flashing marquees of clubs with names like "The Man Hole" and "Men At Work." Rainbow flags flew from virtually every business, their doorways partially blocked by stacks of magazines with beefy men on the covers. There were even condos that catered to a nearly exclusive gay clientele. On a windy winter night, I found myself sitting in one. It was owned by my first creative writing professor, Edward Homewood; he had invited me and two other students from our community college to dinner. We'd consumed four bottles of Chardonnay and now sat in the living room chain-smoking and nibbling cantaloupe wrapped with prosciutto, getting to know each other. The subject of relationships was raised. Someone, Vicky, I think, asked me if I was dating.

I nodded.

"Is it a he," Tony asked, "or a she?"

"A she," I responded.

He frowned. "How disappointing."

"*Very*," agreed Professor Homewood. And then he told a story I would hear maybe a dozen times over the next fifteen years; two elderly men were sitting on a bench feeding pigeons, when one of the men confessed his lifelong love for the other. The other responded by crying, since the feeling was mutual and they had spent the last sixty years as mere friends. When Professor Homewood finished telling this story, he lit another cigarette and scanned our faces. "Avoid sitting on such a bench," he warned, "at all costs."

"The gay bench of regret," added Vicky, an aspiring poet. "I like that."

"But what if," I asked, "what if the second man wasn't gay?"

Professor Homewood shook his head emphatically. "There is no such man. Or woman, for that matter. We are all gay. We are all straight. Some people, those residing at the peak of Mount Darwin, are simply more in touch with their full selves than others."

I thought about this for a moment. "So, you could fall in love, romantically, with a woman?"

"*Me?* God, *no.*"

Vicky, Tony, and I looked at each other, then back at Professor Homewood.

"I am, in terms of sexual evolution," he said, "a slug."

Tony patted my knee. "But *you*," he said, "could be romantic with a man. And my plan is to prove it to you."

He tried very hard. He flirted with me, complimented my clothes, brushed his leg against mine when he, Vicky, and I sat in dark movie theaters. He bought me meals. He even got jealous, on occasion, as if the mere fact of his plan had made us a couple. Once, a year into this plan, he snapped at a man who had offered to buy me a beer. We were in a gay bar.

"You may *not*," Tony told him, "do any such thing."

The man nodded and tipped his cowboy hat. It was rodeo night. Banjo strumming and hoots filled the air. "No offense," the man said. "I didn't know you two were together."

Tony shouted, "Well now you know, buckaroo!" He was drunk. So was Vicky. So was I. Earlier that day she and I had watched Tony break down as he told us his boyfriend had left him. He'd found Vicky and me at our usual coffee shop, where we sat by the window trembling from triple cappuccinos. We all needed a drink. Tony said he knew just the place. We stopped at a drugstore and purchased three red bandanas, tied them around our necks, and then went to Halsted Street to enter the wild wild west. That was three shots and twenty beers ago. Soon after the man had offered to buy me a drink, Vicky leaned toward me and whispered, "I think I'm going to vomit."

"In that case," I said, rising, "we should go."

How could mid-January be so warm! Even with so much snow and ice, so much wind! Reveling in this climactic miracle, we locked arms and decided to walk. An hour later, just as our terrible sobering was complete, we entered Vicky's apartment. It was a studio, minus the bathroom and kitchen, which were down the hall. The only furniture was a day bed and a blue easy chair. "Dibs on the chair," Tony said. He flopped down and began removing his shoes.

"You and I can sleep together," Vicky said to me. "It'll be a tight fit, though."

I was already anticipating my girlfriend's wrath for being out all night. A tight fit on a daybed with another woman did not seem like a good idea. "I should leave," I said.

"Aw, come on," Vicky coaxed.

"My girlfriend, she's going to kill me."

Tony rolled his eyes.

"Call her." Vicky took the phone off the receiver and held it out to me. "Tell her where you are."

But it would have been no use. My girlfriend was annoyed about how much time I spent with them, the subject of several fights. Besides, I had told her I would be at her place by 10 p.m., nearly three hours ago.

I removed my bandana, stuffed it into my pocket, and turned to leave. Vicky joined me at the door. We shared a long hug. As we parted, she kissed me on the mouth. It was a mere peck, as a sister might give a baby brother, a mother to her young son, but it was something we had never done before and caught me by surprise. Now Tony rose and approached me, his arms extended. I suspected he would try to kiss me too, but after we embraced he turned to walk away. I pulled him back. The look of shock on his face after our lips parted was priceless. It stayed with me during my long walk home, and it came to mind when my student's father asked me if I had a thing for gays. I thought of Crystal then, and of Professor Homewood. I even thought of my childhood friend Paul. "Not all of them," I said. But yes. I have loved a few.

BREATHE

One cause of your son's seizure, the doctor says, could be syphilis. Ask what's the basis for such speculation, given that no physical exam was conducted, no blood work drawn, no urine sample taken, and that your son, who is lying on the hospital bed before you looking bewildered, is twelve. "Obviously it's not unheard of for twelve-year-olds to have this disease," she responds, which is impossible for you not to hear as, "You're black, so I shouldn't have to tell you this."

But it is possible, apparently, not to lose your temper. Be grateful for the article you read last month about the benefits of breathing exercises in times of high stress because the one you're doing now is actually working. Before speaking, take another deep breath, followed by a slow exhale, focusing, all the while, on the air passing through your lungs. There. Now tell your family it's time to leave. Marvel at the calmness of your voice and wish you'd discovered this exercise years ago, long before your high blood pressure and reputation for being angry. Pat your son's shoulder as you nudge him upright. Take him home.

Once home, in your study, do some google searches. Start with syphilis. Tell yourself you know your son doesn't have syphilis but be curious to see if the doctor was racist and dumb or only racist. Find it hard to decide; syphilis left untreated for a decade can cause meningitis which can cause seizures. Forget the doctor and just search "adolescents and seizures" but when you reach the part about brain tumors turn off the computer and work on your breathing some more. Come up with your own diagnosis; the seizure was a fluke, a random occurrence, like hiccups or warts. Try to convince yourself there's no need to worry.

There is need to worry, though, because your wife is in the kitchen screaming. Run there to find her standing next to your son, who is seizing again, his thin quivering arms bent at odd angles like a scarecrow's. Choke up tomorrow as you recall how your ten-year-old gently placed a hand on his brother's lower back to steady him but for now keep it together. You need to be strong. You need to be wise too, which is problematic; the seizure has run its course and your son looks at you with fear in his eyes and says, "Daddy, why is this happening?" You cannot answer this. Believe a good father could. A good father, if you think about it, would not have bought a house in a small white town so that when medical emergencies arise paramedics take you to the nearby small white hospital instead of to Boston, thirty miles away, where the world's best hospitals receive black people all the time. And a good father would have just said, "We're driving him to Boston Children's," before his wife beat him to it. Agree with her, at least. At least get the phone so she can arrange a sitter.

to do it once more, and we were not in a courthouse, and I was not yet simple.

I leaned toward him. "I did it," I whispered. "I'm sorry."

"I know, son," he said. "That's why you're here." And then he told me, as he had several times already, "Just let me do the talking." We were halfway down the aisle now, the red tip of his cane sweeping across the floor. The room had fallen quiet, with everyone staring at us intensely and seemingly without breath, including the judge. He was elderly, bald, with glasses perched on the crown of his skull, and he wore a mustache that obsessed him. During the hour we had sat there I had watched him fiddle with the upturned ends, alternately twisting each side between a forefinger and thumb. He did this for a number of seconds when we reached him before picking up a sheet of paper, lowering his glasses, and reading the charges. When he finished, the bailiff called the witness. I glanced over my shoulder to see who would come forward. No one did. The bailiff repeated the witness's name. Still no one moved.

The judge looked down at me, his hand rising to his mustache. "It appears that today could be your lucky day, Thomas."

"I'm not Thomas," I told him.

"You're not?"

My father released my arm and inched forward. "I am, Your Honor."

"*You're* Thomas Walker?"

"Yes."

"Thomas, this may be a dumb question, but aren't you *blind?*"

"Yes, Your Honor."

"And I take it you were blind three weeks ago, when this crime occurred?"

It is Saturday, shortly after 9:00 p.m. Very few cars are on the highway. Conclude, in other words, that there's nothing to prevent you from showing your resolve to get answers by driving ninety miles an hour, except for your wife, who thinks she can do so by calling you a lunatic. She can't. She doesn't even know what a genuine lunatic looks like. Let a cop stop you; then she'll know. Just let one stop you. Let a white cop stop you, damn it. A white cop, with some weird-ass sunburn in December, probably, and his mouth full of tobacco. Between the tobacco and a southern drawl you will barely understand him ordering you to step out of the car, *boy*, and keep your hands where he can see them. He'll see your hands, all right. He'll see them as they're going upside his goddamn head . . .

Snap out of it. You're getting worked up and so is your wife, who's now demanding you to slow down. Go ahead and do it and while you're at it remind yourself that stress kills. You don't want to end up like your father, after all, who only lived to be sixty-eight, although that was much longer than one of your brothers, who only made it to forty-seven. You've outlived your brother by two years but outliving your father will be harder. You are even more high-strung than he was, a trait greatly exacerbated by fatherhood, or rather by the inadequacy fatherhood often makes you feel, especially when you think of your duty to protect your sons from harm, including, needless to say, racism. You think of this duty all the time. Lately, when thinking of it, your mind plays tricks on you by swapping out your sons' faces with the face of Travyon Martin, the recently slain black teen. When this happens your breathing exercises do not work. They only work on things like being told your twelve-year-old has syphilis.

It's 10:15 when you arrive at Boston Children's. Even at this hour the place is packed. Fill out some paperwork at the receptionist's desk and then sit in the waiting room with dozens of other people, many of whom are black, which is good to see, but wish they were not here. Wish there were no white people either. Or Asian. That woman and infant of dubious ethnicity can stay because there are only two of them but in a perfect world they would not be here either. The bottom line is you'll be here a while, maybe all night, unless, that is, your son has another seizure. Hope that he does. A brief one. No more than ten seconds or so, just long enough to get the receptionist to call a triage. Or maybe he can fake a seizure. That would be better, now that you think about it, since who knows what kind of damage the seizures are causing his brain, or who knows, as you think about it more deeply, what kind of brain damage is causing the seizures.

If he has brain damage that's not a tumor assume it occurred at Mercy General, another small white hospital, where your wife's seven-hour labor culminated in him being stuck in her birth canal. The doctor held off for so long to have a C-section that it became more of a life-threatening proposition than continuing to try to suck your son out with a vacuum. When the vacuuming presented itself as the greater threat, an emergency C-section was ordered, but right before your wife was rushed to the OR the doctor made one final attempt, yelling *push, push, push* as you whispered *please, please, please* and with that your son plopped free with a blue face and his head smushed into a cone. Now he's having seizures. And now, unlike then, when you wept with gratitude while hugging the staff, let this thought enter your mind: if your family had been white, a C-section would have been performed at the first sign of trouble.

"Are you okay?" your wife is asking.

"I'm fine."

"Then why are you doing your breathing exercise?"

Tell her it's precautionary. Tell her that even though Boston Children's is one of the world's premier heath institutions, the doctor you get could be a screwball, a real nutjob who somehow slipped through the cracks, and then notice your son's wide eyes and realize this was the wrong thing to say. Put your arm around his shoulders. Tell him not to worry. Assure him that the doctors here are as sane as you are and that, if he wants this proved sooner rather than later, he must fake a seizure. He chuckles, because he thinks you are joking.

Two hours pass before a nurse calls his name and leads your family to an examination room. After she takes his vitals, your wife describes the seizures from earlier today before mentioning another, the one that occurred when he was two because, you later learned, of a temperature spike. You hadn't thought of that for some time but the memory returns with awful clarity, the way his body went rigid as you were buckling him into his car seat, how his eyes rotated in their sockets until only white remained. You yelled for your wife to call 911 and while you were snatching your son into your arms you pictured your father, who was epileptic, thrashing about on the floor with blood oozing from his mouth as he involuntarily bit his tongue. You will never forget that blood. You were still thinking of it when the paramedic admonished you for risking being injured by forcing a finger between your son's clamped teeth, but you knew, if necessary, you would do it a thousand times more. You would have done it today. You would have, but all your son did was tremble, his mouth slack but also—as if he were trying to keep you from stressing out, from completely losing it, from dropping dead like your brother of a massive stroke—fixed into a sad little smile. You will never forget that sad little smile either.

Your wife finishes giving his medical history. The nurse, before leaving, says a neurologist will be in shortly. Wonder what she meant by that two hours later. Your son is asleep. You are angry. Your wife is legendary for her patience but she is getting angry too. Do not bother suggesting she join you in doing a breathing exercise because when you first mentioned its benefits she said it was not for her. It is for you, though. It's helping you stay alive. Decide that all it needs is a modification. Leave the room.

There are no nurses at the nurses' station but two clerks are sitting there talking. When you reach them, inhale deeply, and then slowly exhale. Do this once more. Now tell them you have been waiting to see a doctor for three goddamn hours. Tell them this is unacceptable, this is some *bullshit,* and then insist on seeing someone *right now,* just as you should have insisted that the paramedics bring you here and you should have told that syphilis doctor to fuck herself and you should have, all those years ago, demanded a C-section as soon as there was trouble. The clerks are speechless. They look aghast. They are staring at you with gaped mouths as if you're a lunatic but they have no idea. You could show them what a real lunatic looks like. You definitely could. Instead, as you back away, show them more deep breathing.

A moment after you return to the room a doctor bursts in, already apologizing. There was a mix-up, he says, at the change of shift; no one informed him that you were here. Maybe this is true, maybe it's not. Decide for the time being it doesn't matter. All that matters is that he's here now and your son is having seizures and you want to know why.

In five days you will. One referral will lead to another which will lead to a diagnosis of Paroxysmal Kinesigenic Dyskinesia, a neurological disorder that can trigger petite seizures when the body is suddenly thrust into motion. It strikes pubescent children and can last through their late teens or early twenties. It's a rare disease, largely unknown to the medical profession, and next week, standing before you in this very room, as fate would have it, will be the neurologist credited with its discovery. There are medicines to control the seizures, he will say. He will say everything will be fine. The neurologist standing before you now does not say everything will be fine, but he knows enough, after thoroughly examining your son, to say this: "The seizures themselves, while frightening to experience, and no doubt even more so for parents to witness, are harmless."

Look at your wife and son. See how their faces have broken with relief. Yours has too, but only for an instant before stiffening again, the result of another modification you add to your breathing exercise. From this point on, whenever you are under high stress, after you have blown off a little steam between deep breaths and slow exhales, think of something you have done, as a father, that is worthy of the title. Right now think, once again, of your son's first seizure. Picture yourself clutching his rigid little body. See yourself staring into the void of his eyes. "I'm here, I'm here," remember whispering, as his teeth bore into your skin.

THE HEART

For a decade my twin brother struggled to save his marriage, but late one winter night he accepted that it was over, right after his wife nearly cut off his thumb. It dangled from a strip of flesh while his wife, still holding the butcher knife, flailed around in a spasm of remorse. He moved to console her, insisting that everything would be OK, displaying the kind of humanity perhaps common only in people who believe they can wed heroin addicts and have things turn out well.

She was, needless to say, high at the time. Jim, for his part, had had a great deal to drink, but he wasn't drunk, alcohol for him having become, over the better part of his thirty-eight years, more of a stabilizer than an intoxicant. His refrigerator was always full of malt liquor, 40-ounce bottles stacked neatly on the bottom shelf like an arsenal of small torpedoes. There was a lone bottle chilling in the freezer; he had been just about to remove it when his wife tore into the kitchen, grabbed a knife from the drawer, and accused him of being unfaithful. She frequently displayed this sort of wild paranoia, though it is true that earlier in the day he had flirted with one of the moms at a birthday party he had attended with his two daughters and son. His daughters were six and seven; his son, five. Now, having been awakened by their mother's shouting, they stood huddled together at the top of the stairs, quietly watching as she retrieved a plastic baggie from one of the drawers and proceeded to fill it with ice from the freezer, a remarkably astute response, given the circumstances. She even had the presence of mind to remove the bottle of beer from the freezer, lest it be forgotten and explode, as others had before. She offered it to Jim. He declined, on account of being busy holding his thumb together. She pressed the bag of ice against the wound and began wrapping it in place with a drying towel. Seeing them standing so close together, my brother's back pressed against the stove, a stranger entering the room might have mistaken this scene for something other than what it was—at least until after the thumb was wrapped, when Jim reached for the phone to call 911. "My wife," he said when the operator answered, "fucked me up."

The operator requested that he be more specific. He explained what had happened. Her voice heavy with boredom, as if my brother's predicament were a common one, or simply low-ranking on the crisis scale, the operator told him to keep his hand elevated until the EMTs arrived. When she advised him to keep the thumb cold, Jim felt a surge of appreciation for his wife, for the way she had moved to preserve his finger was an example of how caring she could be. Deep down inside, she was a good person; he'd never doubted this. On the surface, unfortunately, was a troubled soul, which—despite his love for her—simply would not, and maybe could not, be soothed.

This realization was long in the making, having been delayed by periods of sobriety, when she was soft-spoken and kind. He had met her during one of those periods. They were both studying for their GEDs, trying to reroute lives gone off track, because she didn't *have* to be on welfare forever, and he didn't *have* to always be a hospital orderly. So there they were, taking a class at the local community college, where she sat at the desk to his left, her body petite and fidgety, her skin the color of coffee beans, making it difficult to see, in her arms and legs, the tracks that he'd later tell her didn't matter. It was his unconditional acceptance of her that lengthened her abstinence longer than it had gone before, a full six months, so that when her relapse finally arrived, boring down on him like a massive hurricane, he'd already taken shelter in that area of the heart where reason does not venture. It was while there, no doubt, that he'd decided to marry her.

Our family had struggled to make sense of this decision. Sometimes, when we spoke of it in his absence, we offered the kind of pop analyses one would find on a daytime talk show, using phrases like "low self-esteem" and "nurturing complex," and then, exhausted by the futility of this exercise, I would simply hope for her to overdose and die. It was an awful thing to do; I understood that long before it finally happened. He called with the news of her passing as I was about to prepare for class, though I abandoned that plan to assuage my guilt. She clearly had a death wish, I told myself; I'd merely wanted it to be fulfilled without also including my brother. From the moment they married I'd feared receiving the phone call that would announce their bodies had been found in their bed, each containing a single bullet in the manner of murders involving unpaid debts. Because while it had reached the point where he was *giving* her money to get high, he could never give her enough, so she was driven to find it by other means. Often, this required dealing with the kind of people who would hold you hostage, forcing you to perform sex acts with men clutching twenty-dollar bills until the account was settled—that happened to her more than once. It happened, too, that thugs showed up at their house looking for her; threatening messages were left on their phone. So, yes, I'd wanted her to die. Instead, she gave life. Three children in three years, each one born premature, and each one, like her, addicted and pleading for help.

One of them made a plea after the stabbing. It was their son, whose own thumb was crammed in his mouth, making him difficult to understand when he begged his mother not to hurt his father.

His parents pulled apart. "What are you doing up?" his father asked. "Go back to bed. All of you, *scat.*"

"But we heard yelling." That was the six-year-old.

The seven-year-old added, "And we saw daddy's finger! It's bleeding!"

"Go back to bed, damn it," shouted their mother, "before I make *y'alls* fingers bleed!"

Regardless of the effectiveness of the threat (the children fled to their rooms without another word) Jim felt it was uncalled for. But there was no point in his saying so because she was gone, replaced again by the addict who had thrust a knife towards his belly. It was the addict who yelled: *None of this would have happened if you hadn't been messing around with some hussy!* And: *You think I don't know what the hell you been doing all day?* And also: *You lucky only your* thumb *is on ice, motherfucker!* It was the addict who scampered from the kitchen into the living room, from the living room to the dining room, from the dining room to the kitchen, over and over, like a panther in a cage.

But it was the woman he loved who came back, crying now, professing her sorrow, cursing her life, wishing she'd never been born and then wrapping her arms around his waist, tilting up her head to snuggle her runny nose against his neck, and for an instant—but only for an instant because this thought was interrupted by the blare of approaching sirens—he believed he could still make their marriage work.

Outside, the street swirled in festive lights, celebrating its end.

BALLING

A private college in Boston was making headlines for all the wrong reasons. Along with being criticized for its lack of racial diversity, one of its black faculty had filed a discrimination lawsuit, and another had complained to the Massachusetts Commission Against Discrimination. A third had quit. It was rumored that the president, under whose watch these troubles festered, was being forced to resign. And so when I saw their ad for a professor of creative writing, with a specific appeal for applicants of color, I could not believe my good fortune. The college, it seemed to me, like a flowering boll of cotton beneath the hot Georgia sun, was ripe for the picking.

A flowering boll of cotton would have been too much to ask for, but I could have used some hot Georgia sun. My complexion was its usual mid-New-England-winter pale, and I feared that competitors for the job with darker skin, even if by only a shade or two, would have a psychological edge with the search committee. I had first seen this sort of thing as a child; on basketball courts, as players were being divvied up into teams, the darker your skin, the greater the assumption that you were a baller. I was routinely chosen near the end, or left on the sidelines entirely, being that I am closer in hue to a banana than a plum. As I grew older I noticed that this assumption extended to other areas of life, such as the ability to dance, to fight, and to copulate with great skill and endurance; surely it had reached a private college in dire need of some Negroes.

Morally speaking, I am not a perfect person—who is?—so I considered getting a tan. There was a salon next door to the Starbucks I frequented and sometimes, before getting out of my car to grab a cappuccino, I would see ghostly Caucasians enter its doors and their dazzlingly bronzed counterparts exit. I imagined going inside and how the clerk, after initially being confused by my presence in the lobby, would open the cash register and dump its contents on the counter, right after pressing the silent alarm. But that could work in my favor; few things evoke more sympathy for a black man than his false arrest. "Traffic into Boston was slow going," I could tell the hiring committee, "but I'd rather be sitting on I-95 than in a jail cell, as I was last week." If only life were that simple. Any sympathy gains would be lost once I combined in a sentence the words "lobby" and "Tanorama." The sad state of my complexion would have to remain.

My attire, however, was definitely in play, as O. J. Simpson's had been during his trial for murder. I remembered how he would come to court wearing kente-cloth ties and earth-toned suits, which for O. J., who had long ago rejected all things related to black culture, were the equivalent of dashikis and boubous. I think he even occasionally wore a pin of Africa on his lapel. Just as I had begun to wonder if he would don a fez, it was rendered unnecessary by the testimony of Mark Furman. As it turned out, the college where I currently worked had its fair share of Mark Furmans; that, however, was not why I wanted to leave. I wanted to leave because private colleges pay considerably more than state colleges. If winning the job meant putting one or two of my Mark Furmans on the stand, I would not hesitate to do so.

The ad called for the standard fare: evidence of good teaching, experience working on committees, and a strong record of publication, including a book. Of these, the book was most important, and mine was forthcoming. It was a memoir about my experiences as a collegiate, husband, father, and academic, but it included many anecdotes from my teenaged years in a ghetto, which meant I was golden. I simply had to play up the ghetto parts, as had the publisher, who adorned the cover with prostitutes, hoodlums, and a driverless Cadillac, its owner, presumably, bound and gagged in the trunk. Now I was grateful that my objections to these images were not heeded. I was grateful, too, that there had been no enthusiasm for my working title, *The Mechanics of Being.* "It's a nod to my mentor James Alan McPherson," I explained, "who urged black writers to move beyond complaining about racism to addressing the universality of the human condition." "Too Zen," the publisher replied. Zen, she noted, was the very opposite of African American. She changed the title to *Street Shadows* and planned to release the book in February to coincide with Black History Month, which, as fate would have it, coincided with the deadline for the job applications. All stars were aligning in my favor.

But first things first: I needed a strong cover letter. Academic positions can be won or lost in their opening paragraph, nay, with their very salutation, which is why I deleted "*As-Salaam-Alaikum*" as soon as I typed it, as it could be seen as pandering. "Dear Search Committee," I wrote instead, "As an African American with experience teaching African American literature, including slave narratives, *Native Son*, and Toni Morrison, and whose memoir, *Street Shadows*, chronicles my experiences as a black teen in a Chicago ghetto, I believe I am particularly well-suited to meet your college's needs." I read it to Brenda.

"Are you trying to not get the job?" she asked.

"Quite the contrary."

"Then I suggest you stop pandering."

I snorted. "This isn't pandering. Pandering would be greeting the committee with, say, *As-Salaam-Alaikum.*"

"No one's dumb enough to do that," she said. "But you *are* pandering."

"Actually," I explained, "I'm balling."

"What?"

I told her about being picked last at hoops.

"Maybe you just weren't any good."

It was true that my crossover needed work, as well as my defensive skills and rebounding. I had a decent mid-range jumper, though, given the right opponent, like "Little" Tommy Jones, or his baby sister. But I did not argue the point. The key to balling was improvisation, after all, having the agility to perform whatever act a specific moment required; for now the shrewder move might be merely to identify rather than emphasize my race. What I emphasized were my awards for teaching and service, my two terminal degrees, a comprehensive list of the intellectual and creative strengths I felt I could bring to the institution, and my publications and forthcoming book. I doubted the wisdom of this approach for the month it took the search committee to call. My interview was scheduled for March.

That gave me two months, more than enough time to buy the books of the creative writing faculty, though not enough time to read them. So I merely skimmed their contents and memorized the author bios. I memorized the authors' faces too, one of which came easily, a black female writer-in-residence. At first she struck fear into my heart, as it dawned on me that the search was a farce designed to promote her to the tenure track, but ultimately I decided she was one of the plaintiffs; there was just something about her coy smile that signaled she had the institution, if not the world, by the throat. It was, I'd bet, a practiced expression.

I practiced my expressions too, avoiding the coy one, so as not to tip my hand. And I shied away from ones that made me look overly friendly, like the Sambos in antebellum movies, or Bill Cosby before he had to switch to sad and confused. Which brought to mind another possibility; maybe I should not smile at all. I could scowl, in the manner of Kanye West, to show I meant business. There was a risk in that, though, since in the eyes of many the business of a scowling black man was assault or murder. The image I wanted to project was of a black man who was proud but not angry, kind but not buffoonish, streetwise yet cosmopolitan, someone who could gracefully diversify cocktail parties as the host's only black friend. By the time the interview arrived, I had watched every YouTube video of Will Smith I could find.

The interview was a daylong affair. First I met with the search committee, which consisted of two white males and a thickly accented woman I identified as Latina, though I later learned she was Greek. There *was* a Latina in the department, however, as well as a Latino, both of whom attended my presentation, along with a dozen other faculty. Two more faculty members interviewed me over lunch; another interviewed me during a campus tour. And then some students, the staff, the chair, and the dean interviewed me in quick succession. None of these interviewers was black, which I found both astonishing and fortuitous. They definitely had a race problem, and I believed I was making a strong case to help solve it. My answers to their questions were rock solid. I was witty and charming. I spoke compellingly about my work. And I responded with genuine enthusiasm whenever someone boasted of the college's attributes, which were plentiful. It truly was a fine institution, so it must have been humiliating to have its reputation marred by the public airing of its racial discord, while most colleges and universities manage to keep theirs under wraps. No one I had spoken with broached this subject, however. Nor had I.

But was that the best strategy? I had wondered about it constantly in the weeks leading up to the interview. Inquiring about their race problems could show I was candid and mature enough to discuss such a sensitive topic. On the other hand, it could come across as crass and tactless, maybe even accusatory. By the time I was led to the office of the Vice President for the final interview, I still was not sure what to do.

The first fifteen minutes were formal as she peppered me with questions, occasionally interjecting positive references to my resume, or describing hypothetical courses I would be asked to develop. And then the conversation turned informal, touching on current events, sports, and even fashion, as she noted her admiration of my kente-cloth tie. But as the interview wound to an end, her demeanor suddenly tensed. "We've had some problems with diversity," she said, as she leaned back in her chair. "Perhaps you've heard?"

"Yes," I replied. "As a matter of fact, I have."

"I hope that hasn't dampened your opinion of us. We're not a bad institution," she stressed. "We're just experiencing some growing pains. Maybe your college is as well?"

She was seeking to establish a kinship, I knew, one based on the difficulties of navigating matters of race; that was my cue to call my Mark Fuhrmans to the stand, and I could start with the colleague who feared I would physically assault her. "These kinds of growing pains," I said instead, "are hallmarks of the universality of the human condition, and all institutions, like all individuals, must undergo them as we improve as a society." Her face softened into a smile, and I knew the job was won. How could it not be? I had just hit her with a sweet crossover, after all, one so deft that she never saw it coming.

TESTIMONY

I'd always wanted my sons to have a firsthand appreciation of basketball, in part because it embodies the kind of
heroic values that for centuries have sustained our race,
such as drive, improvisation, and poise under pressure.
But when Dorian was two I made an errant pass to the
back of his head, knocking him to the cement driveway
and busting open his chin, after which his and Adrian's
love of the game failed to blossom. They have an appreciation for my stories, though, so maybe it will be enough,
when they are a little older, to tell them about the street
tournaments I watched as a teen.

The games started at sunset, but by noon the crowd
would already be a few dozen strong. There'd be cool-
ers full of beer and, to ward off Chicago's vicious mosqui-
toes or a nasty fall chill, trashcans full of fire. Someone
would have brought a boom box, its speakers vibrating
like war drums to the beat of The Ohio Players. By the
game's end, if there had not been any violence, the fes-
tivities would have produced a few cheerleaders, women

over fifty who still remembered being graceful and some who had entirely forgotten, like Mrs. Dean, who fell once and sprained her wrist after only one lackluster spin.

It was October when Mrs. Dean got hurt, just after the final game of the 1980 season, when I was sixteen. Our only active legend on hand was June Bug. Big P. had died of a heroin overdose and Hunter was in jail. Rumor had it that when Hunter climbed through the shattered window of a dry cleaners, three fur coats under each arm, he squinted past the glare of a flashlight, recognized the guns aimed at him were being held by detectives Stickman and Cowboy, and said, "Y'all realize the big game is Saturday?"

"Damn, that's right," said Stickman, as he and his partner lowered their weapons. "This Saturday or next?"

"This one."

"You still on parole?"

"Two more months."

"How's your jump shot?"

Hunter grinned. "Sinking like battleships, *baby*."

Cowboy nudged up his Stetson with a forefinger and said, "Okay, Hunter, get out of here." Hunter smiled and began to walk away, stepping lightly on the broken glass, and then pausing to turn when Stickman called his name and told him to leave the fur coats. Hunter complied before going straight to White Castle for five cheeseburgers, a large root beer, and to rob the teller. The officer who caught him this time did his duty. His unwavering adherence to the law, in addition to his failure to inquire about Hunter's jumper, confirmed a rumor that his nephew played for the opposition.

"That's his nephew right there!" A finger in the crowd directed us to one of the players, the fat one waving the money. "Your uncle," someone yelled, "is a *snitch*!" The cop's nephew ignored him. He waved the money some more, calling us out, taunting us. His teammates stood off to the side stretching their calves and hamstrings, cigarettes bobbing between their smirking lips, and their fans, who'd arrived in a six-car caravan, began to egg us on. June Bug finished his beer. He swaggered forward with his thumbs hooked on the front of his blue shorts. Four young players he'd handpicked followed him. The teams met at center court. Someone reached for the boom box; the volume on The Ohio Players fell.

"So," grinned the nephew, "where's Big P. and Hunter?"

"Devil got one of them," June Bug answered. "Your uncle got the other."

"I ain't *got* no uncle."

"Yeah, you do," came from the crowd, "and he's a snitch!"

"Listen," the nephew said, "y'all come here to ball or some name calling?"

"Both," June Bug responded. He unhooked a thumb from his shorts and jabbed it over his shoulder. "Me and my boys ready to put a *whipping* on y'alls' monkey asses."

The nephew held up his money. "These two Grants say you won't."

"You're on."

Other bets were made. The referee, a local reverend whose occupation presumed neither objectivity nor fairness, collected the money. He was a former blacktop legend himself and it was for this reason alone that he was trusted. His fanny pack full of bills, he walked onto the court and led a pre-game prayer. Then hands were shaken, the whistle blown, the ball pitched high in the air.

It was a rout from the start. We shouldn't have been surprised, considering the absence of Hunter and Big P., and the fact that one of June Bug's players, dressed in matching red wrist bands and padded knee protectors, which should have tipped us that his game was weak, missed every shot he took. When we were twenty-three points down with five minutes to go, June Bug called a timeout. He pushed his way through our side of the now agitated crowd, stopping several yards away where, leaning against a crabapple tree, a lone man stood smoking reefer.

"Want to play?" June Bug asked.

Buggy did not respond. Most of us weren't certain, by then, if he could even talk. All many of us had ever seen him do was chain smoke his dope and shadow box. And there was a period of time when, for no reason at all, he'd come charging at you with a wild look in his eyes, so it was important to be on guard in his presence, as my friend Paul and I were one morning while pitching pennies. We had seen him come out of his house and every few seconds checked to make sure he wasn't headed our way. So far he was preoccupied with a joint, taking several rapid-fire puffs before sending streams of smoke from his nostrils that carried all the way to us, twenty yards away. He was standing in front of the hedge that surrounded his front yard, dressed in a pair of sneakers, blue jeans, and a tight black t-shirt. His Afro was short and uncombed and he wore a scraggly beard. He had developed a gut by then, small and solid, like a woman five months pregnant, but otherwise he was as thin as he was before heading to Vietnam.

"Oh *shit*," Paul said the next time he looked. "He's coming."

"What do we do?"

"Just play it cool. Play it cool."

We continued pitching pennies, complaining when our shots were off the mark and sent the coins into the weedy grass or far from the line. But we kept an eye on Buggy. He'd reach us soon if we didn't run. We'd been running from him for seven years since his return. But we were men now, we'd decided, just like him, only smaller and younger. We were ten.

"We should speak," Paul said. I nodded. We muttered a few greetings, trying the words out, wondering if we'd have the nerve to use them. We glanced at Buggy. He was five houses away; now four. An approaching car nearly hit us as we darted into the street. When we reached the other side, we looked back to see if Buggy was chasing us, but he wasn't. He had stopped to fight the air. He swung in all directions, twisting his body, ducking, dodging, swinging again, punches intended to cause serious harm. They had caused serious harm once when he'd hit a tree. He broke his knuckles and needed surgery. When he returned from the hospital, his left hand was bundled in gauze, a thin metal rod poking out near the thumb, like a sixth finger.

"Let's get out of here," I said. We were standing behind a parked car, near the hood. "Come on, man."

"Hold up."

"Let's go!"

"Why? He's done."

Buggy stood with his arms to his sides. He was breathing heavily and laughing. The joint was still in his hand, unlit now, the smoldering tip shaken loose and dying at his feet.

"You think he won?" Paul asked.

"Must have, the way he's laughing."

"I'm going to ask him."

"I dare you."

"*Hey, Buggy,*" Paul shouted. "*Did you win? Did you kick some ass, bro?*"

He didn't answer. Someone in the distance had started a lawn mower. Buggy looked for it in the sky.

He'd only gotten worse in the six years since. And *this* was who June Bug wanted on his team?

June Bug asked him again. Buggy pulled at his hairy chin and seemed to be considering the offer. We looked at each other with puzzled expressions, and then back at Buggy, who took three fast hits from the joint before letting it fall to the grass. His first step toward the court triggered sporadic laughter, but also, from the old-timers, testimony.

"Before he was sent to 'Nam, that brother could *play*."

"I remember."

"Was scouted by the Bulls while still in high school."

"Could out-dribble you with just two fingers."

"*Two? Nigger,* you mean *one.*"

"Used to shoot them rainbow jumpers—*swish*—damn near every time."

"*I remember. I remember.*"

But those of us who hadn't seen it or couldn't remember found this hard to believe, especially since all he was doing at the moment was trotting up and down the court, looking confused. He didn't call for the ball and didn't seem to want it. Every time someone threw it to him, he threw it right back. We were laughing like crazy. "*Shoot the ball, Buggy!*" someone yelled, and others began to yell it until it reverberated through the crowd, even among the opposition. "*Shoot the ball, Buggy! Shoot the ball, Buggy!*" We chanted and laughed until the game ended, at which point Buggy, a fresh joint already dangling from his lips, resumed his place near the crabapple tree. Money

changed hands and hands were shaken. The volume on
The Ohio Players was raised. Several women clapped to
the beat as they glided to center court. Mrs. Dean, drain-
ing her sixth beer, stumbled toward them.

SMOKE

Make the reservation online but when you reach the restaurant the hostess says it isn't there. She gives the impression it might materialize, however, if you spell your name while she squints at her computer screen, but no luck. Then she has you confirm that you're not confusing *this* location with their *other* location before she resorts to more squinting, at you, this time, perhaps in an attempt to discern if you're the type of black guy who in moments like this suspects racism. Squint back, so she knows the answer.

This works. She whispers into the mic attached to her blouse and seconds later a waitress appears with four menus. She leads you, your wife, and your twelve- and fourteen-year-old sons into the heart of the large dining room where there are a number of unoccupied tables and booths and the ones that are occupied, be sure to note, are with white people, and then continue on toward a set of French doors along the back wall, through which is a small room without people or booths and only five tables. The waitress stops at one, gesturing for you to sit. Don't.

Say you want a booth. She responds with a look that's equal parts offended and confused, as if you've requested a back rub and a donkey. "I'm *sure* they're all reserved," she says.

Tell her one of those reservations is yours. As you take out your phone to pull up the confirmation, ask for the manager. She relays your request into her mic. She's wearing an earpiece so you can't hear the response but after nodding to it she leads you back into the main dining room where there's no manager but rather another waitress. This one smiles broadly and escorts you to a booth next to a large window overlooking a koi pond, arguably the best seat in the house. As you slide your rump across the worn leather, give your sons that grin of yours that says, *Your daddy's a bad motherfucker!*

It's a good thing they weren't with you last night. You and your wife were at a different restaurant then but which like this one was upscale, absent of other black patrons, and it also had an overflow dining room in the rear, where you had been seated, alone. Soon after you arrived, your friends, a white husband and wife, were escorted to your table. The waitress collected the cocktail orders, described two specials, offered bread and dipping oil, and then departed, at which time the husband leaned towards you and whispered, "I see segregation has been reinstated."

"That very thought," you replied, "crossed my mind."

"Well, let's not stand for it."

That thought had crossed your mind too, but it was mitigated by another; your table, at least, would be integrated. "That's alright," you told him.

"I'll get the waitress," he said, rising.

You waved him back down. "No, really. It's not a big deal."

"*Seriously?*"

You looked toward the wives for input but they were incapacitated, as the menu's vast dessert list had caught their eye. You knew what your wife's response would be anyhow. She'd want to stay. Her tolerance for racism was extreme, in your view, which was to say she resisted it only if it were actually occurring, whereas all you required was its possibility. You had known the man you are dining with to require less. "This is *bullshit*," he continued. "Can't you just *smell* the racism?"

Like a goddamn forest fire, you thought, but saying that would have set him off, which in turn would have set you off, and then you both would have been berating the manager when all you were in the mood for were crab cakes and Chardonnay. So you erased the image of burning trees from your mind and exclaimed, "All I smell, to be honest, is the *creme brûlée!*"

Your wife looked up from her menu and said, "Yum!"

The other wife looked up too. "And the pistachio cake sounds divine!"

The husband looked toward the door. "They can move us," he argued. "We passed plenty of empty tables out there."

"Seriously, it's fine."

"Are you sure?"

"Positive."

Negative, though. You stewed about it throughout dinner, even after two other parties (both white; noted) were seated back there too, and then some more when you got home. When your mind tried to move on to happier thoughts you reined it back in by taking inventory of all the times you'd been led to crappy tables and of the less frequent though more upsetting times your reservations

could not be found, which is why you started requesting booths in the first place, as they are often in prime
locations, and why, for purposes of proof, you make all
your reservations online. The inventorying complete, you
closed the book on the matter for now by vowing to never
again sit at a bad table should you be unable to rule out
race as the motive, with one exception: you would over-
look the infraction if it occurred during a family vacation.
Family vacation, you strongly believe, is the one occasion
when it's important to force yourself to have a good time.
In the days leading up to next week's vacation in Miami,
for instance, you've been practicing your big smile and
visualizing yourself using it on the plane while a toddler
kicks the back of your chair, and when the view from your
four-star hotel is of another four-star hotel, and as a sud-
den cold snap grips the city, requiring you to wear sweat-
ers to the shore.

None of these things happen. In fact, the first seven
vacation days are perfect. On the eighth and final day,
you're in a triumphant mood while strolling along a tour-
ist strip in search of a place for lunch. Settle on a Spanish
bistro less for its promise of tapas than the bright cheery
atmosphere and ample seating visible through the window. Once inside, follow the hostess into and out of the
bright cheery atmosphere and through a narrow corridor that opens to a room with dim lights, black walls and
ceiling, and a low stage, in the center of which is a pole.
At the bar, two elderly men sit hunched over drinks. Acti-
vate your big smile. Say, "Cozy!" As soon as the hostess
leaves, however, your family disagrees. They want to sit up
front. Try to convince them but really yourself that this
isn't so bad before consenting to have your server move
you, should one come. Give it two more minutes, to make

it an even ten, before you rise. When the hostess sees you walking briskly out of the corridor, she takes a step back and mouths *Oh shit!*, as if her last sight on Earth will be of being assaulted by a smiling black man. Bid her a nice day as you leave.

The good time behind you, arrive home prepared to make up for lost ground. Do so the very next weekend by thinking *Aw hell no!* after a waiter escorts your family from the restaurant's crowded, festive first floor to the unpopulated second floor that you believe, with a few downgrades, like swapping out the dozen tables for lockers and replacing the artwork with shelving, would return it to being a storage room. Stop near the top of the stairs and announce, "This is unacceptable." But this time your wife and sons say it's fine. "It *would be* fine," you concede, "if, for some odd reason, we weren't up here *all by ourselves*." Squint at the waiter. Watch his eyes slowly widen, as if you have just pinched a fold of your neck skin and peeled up your face, revealing the one beneath of Martin Luther King, Jr.

The waiter stammers an apology. "I'll go see about getting you a new table," he says. "Please, have a seat. Appetizers while you wait? On the house!" He dashes off and your family sits but before you can give your sons your bad motherfucker grin this happens: another waiter brings up a party of six, and right on their heels is a waiter with a party of three. Both parties are white. The thought occurs to you, even before two more white parties are seated, that they've been bused in. By the time it takes you to eat your roasted red pepper tapenade, the room has become packed with white diners, wholly oblivious, it seems, to the civil rights struggle playing out in their midst. Wonder if you have misread the situation, by which you mean decade.

Your waiter returns, breathless and sweaty. "Sorry that took so long!" he says. "I *finally*, with a little encouragement, if you know what I mean, had a table open up. So," he continues, "if you'll just follow me."

Tell him you've decided to stay.

"Pardon?"

"We'll stay. This is fine."

"Are you . . . are you sure?"

Put the question to your wife. She rolls her eyes. "That's a yes!" you say. Flash the waiter your vacation smile. Be relieved when he returns one just as big but nevertheless expect a little attitude from him now. And don't rule out him doing something unseemly to your food, the prospect of which, combined with the embarrassment you are feeling, will ruin your evening and much of the coming week unless you can make things right. So after he takes your drink orders and walks away from your table, follow him. Trail him down the stairs. Just before he heads into the kitchen, clear your throat and say, "Excuse me." When he turns around, waver in your attempt to rise above yourself and ask for the restroom. He points in its direction, but make no motion toward it. Humble yourself. Do what must be done. "Look," you begin, "I'm sorry for making a fuss about the seating."

"Oh, no need to apologize," he says.

Assure him there is. Appeal to his sense of humanity by offering a glimpse into yours. "It's just that I've been taken to questionable tables in restaurants so often that it's possible, you know, that I've become a little paranoid." Compare it to living near a forest and constantly smelling smoke.

He says, "I totally get that."

"Thank you. I appreciate you understanding."

"No problem," he responds.

Start to leave but stop when he speaks.

"For what it's worth," he says, "after you asked to move and I realized why, I felt terrible. I went straight to our manager and told him we really need to do a better job of taking these kinds of things, things like race, I mean, into account when we seat people. For appearances, you know. At the very least."

Do not hug him. Simply shake his hand. And as you walk back upstairs tell yourself you probably could do a better job, too, of allowing for the possibility of randomness, and of clueless management, and of basic incompetence, to explain a poor dining experience. Allow for these possibilities the next time your reservation is missing. And the next time you are led to a restaurant's former storage space. And when you are taken to a table in an unoccupied overflow room, when your seats abut a kitchen, when your server doesn't return after bringing your food, not even to present your check (you have to ask another server for it), and when you wait over an hour for a reserved table while white diners who arrive after you are seated. But know this: your sons have not seen the last of your bad motherfucker grin, nor, obviously, the measures you'll take to earn it. At some point, when things go wrong, there will be only one logical explanation, the one, to your paranoid mind, that's always in the air.

WARS

I'm greeted in the parking lot by a wiry, elderly woman named Ruth. After thanking me for coming, I assist her in unloading bins of books from her car, stacking them on a dolly. She calls this her "library on wheels," memoirs and novels from her personal collection that she lends to her patients who like to read. I am comforted by both her generosity and the possibility, now awakened, that the resistance to my visit will be less than I feared. She leads me into the Veterans Hospital.

We travel through a maze of corridors before entering a spacious conference room with five seminar tables. Ruth arranges her books on one of them, along with a sign-out sheet, before we sit at an adjacent table and wait for the men. There will be a dozen of them, she explained in her invitation, all of whom experienced combat and now, as a result, lead troubled lives. Some of them are drug addicts. Some are alcoholics. Some abuse their families and others abuse themselves. They would all be required to attend my reading. Not all of them, she warned me, would be pleased about this.

One-by-one they arrive, each carrying a pencil and notebook. If they are unhappy to see me, they express it only by sitting as far from me as they can. But most gather close by and speak quietly with each other until the clock strikes noon. Ruth rises then and, after a brief introduction, I take the floor.

It is an intimidating thing to read to a group of men who have fought in wars—men who have experienced brutality and death with an intimacy few others have or will. I am relatively at ease, though, because I have had intimate experiences with death and brutality too, but never for a moment do I confuse my wars with theirs. Still, I feel a sort of kinship with these men as I read stories of my troubled youth, stories that, by the slightest twist of plot—had I accepted my father's pleas to end my delinquency and joined the military—could have resulted in me sitting where they are, staring stone-faced at a writer holding a book in his slightly trembling hands.

By the time I'm halfway through, my hands have steadied. And their faces have softened, all but one. It belongs to a man who visually fits the stereotype of a Vietnam veteran: middle-aged; black leather vest; bandana tied across his brow; and many piercings—in his ears, his nose, his eyebrows. He's stoned-faced through my every word, and he remains so when I'm done, though by then all the other stone-faces have returned. That's because Ruth has just told everyone to open their notebooks for the writing portion of my visit. The prompt: describe something unforgettable from your youth. She asks if I would like to participate. Sure, I say, why not. She hands me a pencil and a sheet of paper. Because I am here, with these men, I write about Buggy.

It's 1973, the height of summer. I'm nine. For the last ten minutes I've been trapped on the hood of a car, waiting for a chance to make a break for home, or for Paul to discover his eighty-pound German shepherd has gotten free. Whenever one of my neighbors comes outside, I wave my arms and yell, "Milo's loose!" and they hurry back inside. Buggy, however, despite my warnings, casually strolls down his front stairs, sipping from a bottle of Coke. His mother has been saying that Vietnam ruined him, but he looks all right to me, only disoriented and confused sometimes, like there's something he's struggling to remember.

I warn him again. This time he squints in my direction, as if trying to comprehend, or maybe he's just trying to see past the glare of the sun boring into my back. I don't want to be outside anymore. I want to be in my air-conditioned house eating my mother's fried chicken. I hope Milo is hot and hungry too, that at any moment he'll trot off in search of a patch of shade or some food. But for now he's content to sit right below me, exposing the large yellow teeth that, three years earlier, he sunk into my face.

When my brother and I entered Paul's house that day, growls filled the air, which caused Paul to assure us, as he had for the six months we'd known him, that Milo was harmless. So far that seemed to be true. I guess that in part was what gave me the courage to try to pet him, to ignore the bone clamped between his jaws. A short while later I was on a hospital gurney feeling the tug of nine stitches as they closed my cheek and shuddering, as I still shudder nearly a half-century later, from the memory of Milo's lunge.

Buggy takes another sip of Coke. He's stopped in his usual spot—in front of the low hedge that lines his parents' lawn—only twenty yards from Milo and me. I glance around, hoping a squirrel or cat will send Milo off in another direction, away from Buggy, but any chance of that is lost when a belch shoots through the silence and nicks Milo's ears. He snaps his head around. Buggy belches again before lifting the bottle to his lips. Milo darts toward him and stops midway, as if giving his opponent a fair chance to flee. It isn't taken.

Milo torpedoes in low and is met with a kick to his nose. He backs away, barks, and then dives forward, this time getting hold of Buggy's right leg and trying to rip it off. Buggy almost falls but he gathers himself and starts pounding his bottle on Milo's head, Coke spraying everywhere, like celebratory champagne. It takes several more blows until Milo releases his grip. He barks some more before slinking toward his home, his long tail wrapped beneath him, pressed against his belly.

Ruth tells us to stop. She asks for someone to share what he's written. At first no one volunteers, and then hands inch up. The first story is about a mother's cancer; the second is of a father's abandonment; the third, a car accident that claimed the life of a baby brother. And so it goes until we've heard from everyone except for the man with the bandana. Because he sits directly across from me, I saw that, while others wrote, his pencil remained still. The hostess, sitting directly on my left, must have seen this as well. She doesn't press him to participate, though, saying only, after he declines her invitation, that her memory sometimes fails her too. But as he'd held his pencil an inch above his notepad, I saw the expression on his face. It reminded me of what I cannot forget about Buggy's.

After I'd jumped off the car, he watched me slowly approach. When I reached him, he kneeled and pulled up his pant leg; blood covered his shin as it had covered my face. I asked if he was okay. He didn't answer, turning his attention instead to his Coke bottle. It was empty. He frowned and chucked it to the lawn. And then he rose, now looking disoriented and confused, but not, I'd come to understand, like a person struggling to remember. He looked like a person trying to forget.

SIMPLE

It's a difficult pill to swallow when your child falls short of your expectations, even when the expectation is only that he learn to drive. Adrian was showing no capacity for doing so; the three times I had put him behind the wheel in an empty parking lot ended in mutual frustration. "I *told* you I should wait until I'm a little older," he said during our last outing, close to tears. "I'm only *fourteen*." I explained that if I had learned at that age, I probably would not have smashed my parent's station wagon into two parked cars, though I did not mention that, at the time, I was holding a beer in one hand, a joint in the other, and steering with my knee. It was a dumb thing to have done, perhaps the dumbest in all my sixteen years. And then I outdid myself by fleeing the scene.

Twenty minutes later I pulled into our garage to assess the damage. It was as bad as I had feared: a trail of dents and scratches along the passenger side; a dangling rear bumper; two hubcaps ripped free. I wondered if I could get everything repaired without my father ever knowing what had happened, and as I tried to calculate the cost I experienced a rare sense of gratitude that he and my mother were blind. Tired of walking to the grocery store and of relying on friends to ferry them to and from church, my parents had purchased the car and tapped their children as chauffeurs. For the first two years Mary and Tommy had done the chauffeuring. When they left home that responsibility fell to Timmy and Linda, supplemented by Jim and me when we were old enough to drive. It was the four of us, then, whom our parents interrogated when the letter arrived from the Second Municipal District summoning our father, the primary title-holder, to appear before the judge to answer for a hit and run.

The interrogation took place in the dining room. Our father was at the head of the table, our mother at the opposite end. Linda sat next to me. She spoke first. "Daddy, I had *nothing* to do with this."

"Me neither," Jim said.

Timmy, sitting directly across from me, also proclaimed his innocence. As if the matter were settled, my father began folding the court summons, which Linda had read aloud a moment earlier. It seemed that an eyewitness had reported the car's license plate, make, model, and color. "That leaves you, Jerry," my father began, now reinserting the letter into its envelope. "What do you have to say?"

"About what?" I asked.

He held up the summons. "About *this*, Simple." Simple was his new nickname for me. I preferred to think of myself as "fun-loving," but fun-loving people, in his view, did things that resulted in fun, whereas the things I did often led to stitches. There were the nine I received near my lip after I tried to pet Paul's ferocious dog, and the ten I got on my index finger when he and I, pretending to be noblemen and holding pocket knives, proceeded to have a duel. Proving I could punch my fist through a window earned me seven. Once my antics nearly resulted in internal bleeding, as I also proved that I could swallow bleach. And then there were those summer days when I jumped from high rocks into Lake Michigan, despite the sign that warned of rip currents, and the fact that, other than the dog paddle, I could not swim. Sometimes, as I struggled to make it to shore, I could almost hear my father giving my eulogy, concluding it with, "We will miss you, my dear, dear, simple son."

I looked at Timmy; he was making a series of hand and mouth gestures, encouraging me, I assumed, to say I was innocent too. I had told him of the accident shortly after it happened and assured him I had made a clean getaway. But that appeared to not have been the case. I turned back to my father and said, "I didn't do it."

"You didn't do it?"

"No, sir."

"Well, *one* of you is lying."

No one spoke, though my father continued to face me. Were he sighted I imagine we would have made eye contact at that moment, right before he shook his head in disappointment, but it was impossible for him to play his part in that role, and I, as a result, tried never to play mine. I had long since concluded that looking directly into my parents' eyes was a violation of their privacy, and I felt tremendous guilt whenever I fell to the urge. And so now, as I had at various points throughout the interrogation, I willed myself to focus on my father's mouth, which functioned as well as mine and, to my reasoning, put us on equal ground. "I'm not the one who's lying," I said, and then I added, "but I will go with you to the court hearing, if you'd like."

Timmy slapped his forehead.

My father leaned forward in his chair. "You'll go with me to the hearing?"

"Yes, sir."

"Considering you didn't do anything, Jerry, that's awfully generous of you."

I thought I detected an upward turn of his lips, so I smiled and said, "I confess to being an awfully generous person—guilty as charged!" I laughed, though I cut it short when no one joined me.

Later, when Timmy and I were alone, he explained that my willingness to attend court for a crime I claimed to have not committed was tantamount to a confession. He also told me that he had been gesturing for me not to deny committing the hit and run, but rather, in light of the court summons, to come clean and seek our father's mercy. But it was too late for that now. I had to maintain my innocence. And for the next three weeks I did, even when I found myself sitting nervously in court watching defendants approach the bench as free citizens only to be handcuffed and led through a rear door.

"Walker!" the bailiff boomed at last. "*Walker!*"

"Here we go," my father said. We both rose. He took my right arm and we excused ourselves as we inched past several people in the pew. The room was crowded, with upwards of a hundred people, and if all eyes weren't on us already they were when we reached the aisle and my father paused to perform what he once swore to me was magic: he unwrapped the elastic strap that secured the four sections of his cane, held the rubber grip with one hand, and then tossed the three remaining sections forward so that they snapped into place, making a single rod. For a split second my father was a magician again, and I was again a toddler, clapping my hands and begging him

"I was."

"You are the owner of this vehicle, aren't you?"

"I am, Your Honor."

"Please tell me you don't drive it."

I was certain I heard a softening of the judge's tone, a playfulness undercutting his dry delivery, so I said, "Not very well, Your Honor, or he wouldn't have hit the two cars."

The judge looked from my father to me and then back to my father again, whose serious expression remained fixed, whereas mine had already broadened into a grin. When my father's did a second later, the judge burst into laughter, followed by the bailiff, and then laughter filled the room. Even my father joined in. This was a good moment for us, all things considered, a blind man and his simple son bonding in a court of law.

And then the moment got better: the judge dismissed the charges and told us we could leave. My father thanked him. He took my arm, and as we walked back down the aisle, I believed, against all reason, that we would make eye contact and smile.

THE DESIGNATED DRIVER

I arrived at the faculty meeting as a few hundred students stormed the room, chanting about campus-wide racism, demanding justice. Most of the students were white, there to support their black peers as they aired grievances. After a while some of the speakers began to cry, which fueled my growing unease. The offenses struck me as minor, the kinds of slights that I, thirty years ago, as a black student who had also attended an overwhelmingly white university, merely brushed aside, things like coeds requesting to touch my hair, and faculty asking if I were there because of a racial quota. Annoying, to be sure, but not demonstration-worthy, not tear-worthy, not worthy of the bullhorn a young man kept bringing to his lips to shout, "The racism ends *now!*" And each time he did I responded, mentally, that the racism will surely continue, and if you expect to transcend it you will all need to stiffen your spines.

But spines could not stiffen, I conceded, without a certain weight to bear. I conceded, too, that the *weight* of weight was relative; perhaps having white coeds ask to touch your hair today—particularly at an elite, private institution, where one year's tuition costs more than my first home—was the equivalent of being required, sixty years prior, to ride Jim Crow. Maybe sixty years hence, black hair touching would evoke uniform outrage at how inhumanely man once treated his fellow man. I would be long dead by then, so it was a question that would have to be answered by today's youth, including my sons, whose spines, like the spines of the black students before me, were as soft as Jell-O.

Dorian and Adrian were twelve and fourteen. No one had asked to touch their hair yet, though the opportunity abounded, as the town we recently moved to was 98 percent white. It was also wealthy, so it was possible that some of our neighbors attributed our presence to a government program, one designed to ensure a black family per every three thousand homes. No one had asked my sons about racial quotas either. But I worried about how they would respond to questions such as those. I worried about their spines. Having been spared the impoverished, inner-city experience of my childhood, where the social and economic impact of racism was constant and brutal, would they one day find themselves shouting into bullhorns too, aggrieved, say, by the lack of minorities in the cast of *La Traviata,* or their white sommelier's poor choice of Burgundy?

The only racism either of them had experienced occurred a decade ago, when that girl in Adrian's preschool class told him people with his skin color were stinky. The comment was hurtful, but not enduring; within hours he had forgotten it. I, obviously, had not, having instantly recognized the girl for what she was: the fuse leading to the bomb of high school, where the cruelty of four-year-olds met their match in teens. And so when Adrian started his freshman year, I decided to be his designated driver. That way, I reasoned, when he was inevitably embroiled in some racial conflict, our fifteen minutes alone together in the car each morning would be ideal for talking it through.

But eight months had come and gone, and there had been nothing to talk through. It occurred to me, though, while watching the protest, that I could tell Adrian about the students' complaints and then compare them to challenges I had faced in my youth, incidents of police brutality, for instance, or that time I was chased by white teens carrying sticks. It would be a stark departure from our usual discussion of our classes, or the silly dreams I claimed to have had but actually concocted simply to amuse him, but it would provide an important context for dealing with his conflicts to come. So the next morning, midway into our drive, I cleared my throat and said, "There's something we need to talk about." I glanced to my right, just as he dug his hand into the box of Cheerios on his lap, looking, for all the world, like the toddler I once pushed on swings. And then I watched his blank expression blossom into a smile as I made up a dream about our cats fighting and defeating a vulture. I would talk about the protest tomorrow, I told myself. But I did not do it then either.

I did, however, talk about it with my colleagues. It was the talk of the whole college, it seemed, especially after our paper ran it as a feature story. Then the *Boston Globe* and the *Huffington Post* carried it, as well as a few other media outlets, each one highlighting the students' primary demand: cultural competency training for the entire campus community. Most of the faculty I spoke with enthusiastically supported the idea, and it was fun to watch them flinch when I deadpanned that they would have to learn Ebonics. I made this joke several times during the week after the protest, and I was about to make it again at a dinner party with seven of my colleagues, but then someone mentioned how heartbreaking it was to see the students crying and the mood turned somber.

"I could have just hugged the one girl," someone remarked.

"Which one?"

"The one who said the college had broken her spirit."

"Yes, yes. So *sad*."

"But what were they going on about their hair for?" someone else asked. "I couldn't follow that part."

Other than myself and a Cuban American, everyone there was white, so it fell to me to explain that, for some white people, black hair was a great curiosity, compelling them to want to touch it.

"For what purpose?"

"To see what it feels like," I said.

"Really?"

I nodded.

"Have whites asked to touch your hair before?"

"On occasion. But my sisters were asked all the time when they were in college. It's more of a phenomenon among females."

One person said, "How fascinating."

"I had no idea," responded another.

I said, "You'll learn more about it in your Ebonics class."

"Pardon?"

The doorbell rang. One of the guests said it was his wife, who had planned to join us, and a moment after he excused himself he returned with her at his side. I liked his wife. She was from Poland and her perspective on American culture was often unique and provocative. Right now, for instance, after expressions of sympathy for the crying students resumed, she went against the grain by calling them coddled. "That's right," she continued, as my colleagues gaped at her, "coddled."

"How *dare* you say that?" someone exclaimed. "I mean, *how dare you?*"

"I dare," she said, "because it's true. And you're all pathetic for being moved by their petty complaints."

"Their complaints weren't petty," I said, despite my view that they were. But there was something about hearing a white person say it that bothered me.

"Petty complaints," she forged on, "made by coddled babies." Several of my colleagues rose to the students' defense, but she held her ground. "They've probably never experienced *real* racism in their lives."

I leaned forward in my chair. "Wait a minute. Are you saying that privileged black kids are somehow insulated against racism?"

"I'm saying what the students experienced wasn't worth crying about." Then she launched into descriptions of various hardships she had endured in her native land, offering a totalitarian version of the comparison I had intended to give to Adrian. "*And yet,*" she said when she finished, "we didn't cry about it."

"This isn't Poland," I said, "and these aren't your kids."

"Nor are they yours."

"But they *could* be," I snapped, though what I was thinking was that they were. My hands were trembling, I realized, and I tried to steady them by pressing my palms against the table. But that did not work because my Cuban colleague, no doubt recalling the communism of his youth, suddenly announced that he thought the complaints were petty too, triggering a heated argument that got everyone involved. Tempers flared, voices were raised, names were called and, inevitably, accusations of racism were leveled, which brought the argument to an abrupt end.

I rose from the table and went to the patio for some air. A couple of my colleagues joined me with the foresight to bring wine and glasses. For fifteen minutes we drank and expressed our outrage at what we had heard, riling each other up to the point where the thought of remaining at the party any longer was inconceivable. The Pole must have reached the same conclusion; when we filed back inside the hostess was handing her and her husband their jackets. Two colleagues were across the room on the couch, the stark turn of events, I assumed, the source of their stunned expressions. The Cuban was near them on a chair staring into space. He rose when he saw me and gently rested a hand on my shoulder. "Listen," he said, "I don't know how things escalated so fast, but I got caught up in the emotion of it all and I wasn't thinking clearly. I'm pretty sure I offended you, and I deeply regret that. I'm sorry." Smiling faintly, he widened his arms for a hug, which my anger nearly prevented me from accepting. Over his shoulder, the Pole and her husband, jackets on now, said good-bye to the hostess, and then left. A moment later, the remaining guests followed suit.

I was thirty minutes from home. During the drive my anger waxed rather than waned, mainly because I called Brenda and recounted the argument several times over before she told me she was going to bed. She was asleep when I arrived, so I was left to recount it alone for the four hours it took me to finally doze off. When I climbed out of bed an hour later to drive Adrian to school, I was exhausted and irritable.

"Did you have another strange dream?" he asked.

I had just pulled out of our garage and crept toward the busy street that ran by our house. As I waited for a chance to merge into the flow of vehicles, I tried to come up with something, but I just did not have the energy or will. "No," I said. "I didn't really sleep."

"Why not?"

"Too upset."

"With one of your students?"

"No, a couple of friends."

There was a break in the traffic and I pulled forward. For a while neither of us spoke, though mentally I was still at the party, yelling and being yelled at.

"Maybe you should talk about it," Adrian said.

"About what?"

"Why you're upset." He opened the lid of his Cheerios box and inserted his hand. "It might make you feel better."

It would not make me feel better. Besides, to explain the fight I would have to explain the protest, which I did not want to do for fear of being critical of the students, which was to say critical of a future him. But I had to say something or I would have seemed dismissive of his concern. I proceeded with caution and vagueness. "Some students at my college staged a protest," I began. "My friends criticized them, and we argued about it."

"Why were the students protesting?"

"They don't like how they're being treated by some faculty and other students."

"Why did your friends criticize them?"

"They think the students' complaints are petty."

After a short pause, Adrian said, "I'm glad you don't think that."

I wanted to let that stand, as if doing so was no more dishonest than concocting strange dreams, as if he were someone at a dinner party instead of my son. "I do think they're petty," I said, "but the thing is, maybe it doesn't matter what I think. Maybe what matters is what the students think, and the fact that they stood up for themselves. That's not always easy, you know. Actually, I'm proud of them. What they did took courage."

"Like it took for you to defend them," he said.

"Well. . ."

"You should be proud of yourself too, Daddy. I'm proud of you."

I looked at him. He plunged his hand back into the box and pulled out a fist full of cereal. A few of the grains fell to his lap and the floor as he stuffed the rest into his mouth. I turned back to the road, blinking it into focus. In the silence that ensued, my thoughts returned to the party. It was just after the fight, as everyone prepared to leave, and I let myself imagine apologizing to the Pole, as the Cuban had to me. *We have similar views,* I told her, *and I understand the point you were making, but my emotions got the best of me, as they often do when it comes to my sons.* I wished I had said these things to her, and then relayed them to Adrian. *Now* that *was an act of courage,* I could have explained. Not to be confused with an act of love.

STRIPPERS

While at dinner with two friends inquire about the health of their son. He's in stable condition following the chemo, they say, and, at long last, a bone marrow donor has been found. This good news calls for a toast, but now, some toasts later, the restaurant is closing and there are still more toasts to be made. Sympathetic to this dilemma, your waitress suggests the only option nearby, a strip club.

You're not into strip clubs. Even if you were, you'd be ashamed to be seen in one by your students, a real possibility since this club is a block from where you and your friends teach. Also, given the neighborhood's demographics, you'd likely be the only black person in the audience (as you are in this restaurant), and if the strippers were white women there'd be the kind of racial stereotype at play you take pains to avoid. And your wife? She'd be pissed. So bid your friends goodnight and head home—this is what you should have done before the waitress places three complimentary tickets on the table. John picks them up. "I'm game," he says. Maria says, "Me too."

Now is a good time to tell that story about your former professor. "I had this professor once," you begin, "who heard a rumor gay porn was about to be banned. This was in the eighties, I should add, during the AIDS epidemic, when such rumors were to be taken seriously. Anyway, he was still in the closet at the time, so he went to an adult video store a few towns from his to stock up. After he'd put a dozen titles on the counter, the clerk grinned and said, 'Well good evening, *Professor Homewood*! Will these be all?'"

"What did he do?" asks Maria.

"He got a dozen more titles."

"So if any of our students recognize us," John says, "we'll double-down and disrobe."

"*Exactly* my point," you joke, and everyone laughs, but your actual point weighs on you during your walk to the club, slowing your stride, and eventually stopping it. Change your mind about going but then wonder if you're being unreasonable because you only want to toast the good news and that's nothing to be ashamed of no matter who sees you so change your mind back again.

Your feet are slower than your thoughts; Maria wants to know why you're not moving. Make up something. "I'm about to . . . take a selfie."

"A selfie?"

"Yes. For Pam." She's a friend who joined you earlier for a drink. Soon after leaving the restaurant she texted that she'd misplaced her tote bag—and there it was, you saw, beneath the chair where she'd sat, stuffed full of her students' final exams. The loss of those exams would have been catastrophic; thus, her message was all caps and exclamation points. "GOT IT!" You replied. "WILL KEEP SAFE AND SOUND!" In a moment you'll offer her an example of your stewardship, just as soon as you fit the tote into the screen's frame above your head, dangling from a tree.

"Are you done yet?" Maria asks.

"One sec." Snap the photo. Send it after collecting the tote. Don't anticipate an immediate response since it's after midnight, though you've received texts from this friend much later, invariably selfies of her at some outlandish party. She's the kind of person for whom dropping by a strip club would have been a hoot. Wait until she hears where you went tonight. She'll curse herself for leaving.

Your wife, on the other hand, will curse you for staying. Instead of dwelling on that, pay attention to what's happening just ahead at the strip club's entrance. Some men, it seems, are being frisked by a bouncer. What's he searching for? you wonder. Drugs? Knives? *Guns?*

"Final exams," you say. You, John and Maria have been frisked and the bouncer has inquired about the tote's contents. Open and extend the bag. As he reaches a plump hand inside and pokes around, creases form near his eyes and on his forehead, suggesting he believes this could spell trouble. Reassure him by saying you're professors. He opens the door and lets you in.

You're escorted to a corner table by a waiter who looks familiar. A former student? Conceivably, but rule it out because, instead of acknowledging you, all he does is take your orders and leave. Survey the room. It's nearly full. It's dark too, but not so dark you can't make out some faces. They're all white, as you expected, but no one else looks familiar, including the woman on stage, who, naked save platform shoes and bunny ears, is doing something that's a cross between a pirouette and the Hula-Hoop.

"She's not a very good dancer," Maria observes.

John says, "To my great disappointment."

"Well, she's not very *sexy* either."

That's debatable. What's not debatable is her youth. She's twenty, twenty-one tops, the typical age of your undergrads, an association that makes it impossible for you not to wonder about her life. How, for instance, did she come to be on that stage instead of in college? Or maybe she is in college, your college, in fact, and this is the means by which she pays the exorbitant tuition. But most likely she's here as a result of bad choices and bad breaks, although, on second thought, that's a patronizing premise. It could be that being on that stage is her life's ambition. Perhaps she finds the work fulfilling, even liberating, or, at the very least, a satisfactory way to make a buck. There are worse things, after all, than removing your clothes for strangers.

Maria, as if thinking along these lines, mentions her son's illness. The chemo took a great toll on him, she says, and the bone marrow transplant, despite being a blessing, will come with considerable risks. She begins describing one of them, something called graft versus host disease, whereby the recipient's immune system attacks the donor cells, when the bouncer appears at your table. "Miss," he says, interrupting her, "take your feet off that goddamn chair."

Her feet shouldn't be on a chair, granted, but find offense with the manner of the rebuke. Maria does too, apparently; after complying with the order, she says, "*Jesus.* No need to be a *jerk* about it."

"People sit on it, you know," he says.

"Well, *I'm sorry.*" As soon as the bouncer leaves, Maria asks, "What's *he* so uptight about?"

Consider that a rhetorical question, given that his job requires dealing with lechers, some of whom—inebriated, their testosterone primed—are no doubt itching for trouble. At least (thanks to him, actually), they aren't concealing weapons. Which isn't to say that weapons don't abound; know that they do. Recall that story you saw on the evening news about a patron here being stabbed with a broken bottle but resist the impulse to leave. Your drinks have just arrived, after all, and that's the reason you're here. To toast the good news.

Before you can lift your glass, the audience breaks into applause. Look toward the stage; the stripper has finished and is gathering articles of clothing and tossed bills. She has barely ducked behind the curtain when the next performer emerges from its opposite end. It's an older woman this time, in her thirties or forties. She's wearing sheer lingerie and a top hat. She's also holding a cloth and spray bottle. Conclude that her routine is to mime a fancy window washer, until she stops at the pole.

"What's she doing?" Maria asks.

John says, "Disinfecting her work station."

"That's gross," she says.

"Less now, I should think."

"You know what?" she responds. "I've had enough of this dumb place."

"Likewise," John says, reaching for his drink. Maria reaches for hers. Reach for yours. The stripper reaches for one final area of the pole, gives it a spritz, wipes it down, and then begins her routine. Her top hat lends it a delightful touch of merriment, you think, which is in striking contrast to her sneer. This is not her life's ambition. She does not want to be on that stage. Offset the mounting unease you feel about watching her by imagining how she'd feel if you didn't. What could be more demoralizing for a stripper than being ignored? Or for any performer, for that matter? Consider all the times that you, in fact, have felt the sting of disinterest from audience members while giving readings, often of highly personal material. So continue watching her and wish you could be affirmative somehow, that you could offer some positive feedback, though not by tossing money onto the stage, as some crass men are doing, but in a respectful way, a way with class, a way that says, *I truly value you and your work.* When nothing comes to mind, give her a thumbs-up.

Maria leans toward you and whispers, "That's weird."

"What's weird?"

"Thumbs-upping a stripper."

Stop. Try to explain your good intentions but pause mid-sentence when you see, over Maria's shoulder, a woman you think you know. You don't know her, though; it's actually the previous performer. She's wearing a dress now and sitting with a man and another woman. The man, grinning, says something to her. She grins back. The other woman, grinning too, pulls a cherry from her cocktail by the stem and slowly lowers it between her lips. With that, they all rise.

Maria sighs. "This place is boring," she says.

Say, "Maybe not."

"John," Maria says, "isn't this place boring?"

John says he's had better times.

Direct their attention to the woman and the couple, who have arrived at a set of elevators in the far corner. Explain, "That's the first performer, going somewhere with that man and woman."

Maria begins to speak right as the bouncer returns. Her feet are on the chair again. She seems to be just realizing it and quickly removes them.

"I *told* you, Miss," the bouncer says, "to keep your feet off that goddamn chair."

"*Sorry.* I forgot."

"Forgot? What are you, stupid or something?"

"*Hey!*" Maria snaps. "You can't speak to me like that!"

"Who's going to stop me?"

"*He* is," Maria says, pointing toward her husband. "Aren't you, Johnny?"

The bouncer looks at John and snorts. "Is that so?"

"Yes, *it is*," Maria responds. "Go ahead, Johnny. *Stop him.*"

John stumbles to his feet, revealing a detail that heretofore escaped you: he's wasted. Which means Maria and you are too.

The bouncer steps forward. "Is it true, Johnny?" he says. "You're going to stop me?"

John responds with a long, intense stare, as if he's a black belt deciding which arm to break. Or maybe, because he's actually a poet, he's deep in thought, musing on the violent nature of mankind. Either way, accept that he's about to be pummeled.

"Well, Johnny?" the bouncer says.

Maria says, "*Well, Johnny?*"

Well, Johnny, you think, *what have we gotten ourselves into?* Scan the room, as if for the answer, and discover everyone's looking your way. If you have students here who didn't notice you before, they do now. Only be less concerned about that than about being pummeled too, because if the bouncer hits John, who's to say he'll stop there? Who's to say you won't end up in the hospital or in jail or on the evening news?

Then an unexpected thing happens: the bouncer steps back. In a normal voice, a civil one, he says, "Look, we just don't like people putting their feet on the chairs, okay?"

"You're worried about feet on chairs," John asks, "in a *strip club?*"

"I don't make the rules," the bouncer says.

"Oh, *really*? You *don't* make the rules?"

This exchange occurred without John breaking his stare, so he knows it's paying good dividends. He milks it a few seconds longer. Then he abruptly heads for the exit. Maria follows him. Leave money for the drinks and follow her. The patrons you pass turn their attention back to the stage where, you see over your shoulder, the next performer has emerged and is spritzing the pole.

Once outside no one speaks for a while, and when Maria finally does no one responds. "What was *that* about?" she says.

What was *what* about? you wonder. The bouncer's rudeness? His backing down? John's stare? Or maybe she's questioning the decision to go to a strip club in the first place, just as your wife, in the morning, will question too. "What were you *thinking*?" she'll say. "Are you *nuts*?" And that'll even be before you mention thumbs-upping that one performer, like some lecher, or, to be more specific, a black man with a thing for white women. You are neither. You are just a guy who, you'll be ready to admit to yourself by then, used the excuse of toasting good news to see some strippers.

But for now, in this final moment of denial, as you, John, and Maria walk away from the club, try to end the night on a positive note. Say you're grateful no one got hurt. Joke that at least the tickets were free. Express how happy you are for their son. Then, upon reaching the end of the block where you will part ways, stop in your tracks when someone yells, "Professor! *Hey, Professor!*" Feel shame rise in you as you turn, expecting to face one of your students, quite possibly the waiter. It's not. It's the bouncer. He's standing in front of the club, holding something above his head. "Hey, Professor!" he yells again. "Your tote! You forgot these exams!"

THIEVES

Whole Foods shoppers are easy targets, so busy choosing their imported wheat germ and organic kiwi that they forget about thieves. They are also wealthy, at least the ones who live in this town on the shore, where the median home value is a million dollars and the cars are typically high-end, like the Mercedes I park my Toyota next to. I am a good sixty yards from the store's entrance, far enough to complicate a getaway, I note, though by no means making it impossible. Security is light, and the odds of a passerby confronting a running black man are slim.

I prefer coming here mid-morning on a weekday, when it is not very crowded, and that will be especially true now since it has been drizzling for the last hour. Once I am inside, the weather works further in my favor, allowing me to spend several seconds wiping my feet while surveying carts for unattended purses. Right off I see two directly in my path near the apricots. A few feet beyond these, there is another by the corn-on-the-cob. The purses' owners are steps away, their backs to me as they make their overpriced selections. I could have the purses and be gone in a flash. Instead, I remain by the door holding my grocery list close to my face, studying it intensely, offering the possibility that I am a mere dutiful spouse struggling to decipher his wife's scribble.

The corn gatherer isn't falling for it. We've made eye contact and now she returns to her cart, deposits her corn, and then lifts her purse and slips it over her shoulder. The apricot pickers haven't noticed me. I pry a shopping basket from the stack. Against my better judgment, I hurry forward, triggering what I sometimes imagine is an ultrasonic alarm; the two women I am approaching dart glances over their shoulders, seeing me before I have a chance to reach them, and move to secure their belongings.

Another woman—elderly, slightly stooped, light reflecting off the gems squeezing her pudgy fingers—appears at my side, talking about arugula. "You used to keep it by the broccoli," she is saying. "It was there just last week."

"Pardon me?"

"The arugula. Where did you move it?"

"I don't work here," I say.

She looks confused.

"He can probably help you." I point to a man watering daisies. Like all the store employees, he is wearing a brown apron with Whole Foods printed in large lettering across the front. I am wearing a blazer, shirt, tie and stonewashed jeans, a style, according to one of my graduate students, known as smart casual. A prideful part of me wants to mention this to the elderly woman, emphasizing that I am a college professor, but I say nothing as she goes to the produce clerk, who leads her to a field of greens with labels identifying the various species. Perhaps

I only *look* casual and a bushel of arugula will complete the ensemble; the thought occurs to me in jest but nonetheless I act on it.

Next, I get some zucchini, scallions, beets, oranges and bananas, checking each item off my list while working my way to the seafood. There, a man behind the counter, who at most is twenty years old—exactly thirty-one years my junior—nods at me and says, "What's up?"

I reposition the arugula, moving it higher for him to see. Then I bend toward the glass encasement, mainly so he can get a good view of the gray in my hair that, at least with my undergraduates, seems to discourage familiarity. But it does not have this effect on the fishmonger. "Thanks, bro," he says, after filling my request of a pound of Atlantic salmon.

I check my list again. One more item, bread, located on the opposite end of the store. This time I use my phone as a prop, thumbing through emails while being mindful of more purses. I make it past four without tripping the ultrasonic alarm, picking up a bottle of rosemary-infused olive oil in the process, and now I am at the bakery, trying to decide between the pumpkin blue-cheese biscuits and the brioche. And this time my own ultrasonic alarm sounds, causing me to glance to my right where, inches from my elbow, is an abandoned cart with a purse, unzipped, the wallet inside half-exposed like a treasure chest in sand. They belong, I presume, to the blonde five feet away, nibbling at a display of breadsticks and hummus. Before she turns to see what a foolish mistake she's made, I scoop up a brioche and head for the nearest register.

I am third in line. Two customers ahead of me, I realize, is the corn gatherer. She is loading her food onto the conveyor belt, her purse still dangling from her shoulder, her thoughts, I suspect, a million miles from our encounter. Or maybe it never registered at all. Maybe her reaction to me was pure instinct, her body propelled into motion before her mind gave consent. Later, when I am trying to forgive her, this is what I'll decide.

Outside, the drizzle has become a steady rain. Several customers wait for it to abate while standing in the vestibule. I consider doing the same, but I am agitated, as coming to Whole Foods always makes me, and all I want is to be at home. I step through the doors and take off for my car, walking quickly at first, and then, just as I'd imagined, breaking into a run.

ONCE MORE
TO THE GHETTO

We were having trouble getting excited about our trip to Chicago, on account of all the murders. The closer we got to leaving, the more stories there seemed to be of young children gunned down in parks, stray bullets entering apartments and finding mothers making dinner, teens slaying each other without cause. I doubted the city had ever been more dangerous, though a little research proved this to be untrue: during the decade of the eighties, when I was growing up there, Chicago averaged 736 murders a year. In 2015, the year prior to our trip, there were 470. The odds of us making it back alive were much greater than I thought, though not great enough to convince me we would.

One thing we had working in our favor was my familiarity with the city. The murders, I knew, were concentrated in certain communities, so that people who did not live in or venture into them were as likely to be slain as they would be on a Mediterranean cruise. Furthermore, the danger level of these communities varied wildly, often from block to block: some were mere wastelands where abandoned houses outnumbered occupied ones and even muggings were rare, while others were overcrowded and pulsed with all manner of life-threatening activities. Others still were impoverished and crime-ridden yet steeped in working-class values, places mainly populated by law-abiding citizens struggling to make ends meet and to stay out of harm's way. They formed neighborhood watches and threw block parties. They cleaned local parks. They taped handwritten signs in their picture windows that read "Stop the Violence" and "Children at Play: Don't Shoot." These were good people, and I wished they received as much news coverage as the murderers. Maybe then the mere thought of visiting Chicago would not have even someone like me, who *knew* better, wonder about his safety.

The apprehension I felt about the trip manifested itself in Dorian and Adrian as terror. I was to blame for this. Over the years I had shared with them stories about my experience being raised in a ghetto, most of which, not unlike the media's, painted a bleak picture. My intention had only been to stress how lucky they were to live in a town without gangs, for instance, and where their classmates did not bring guns to school. But now each negative news report about Chicago played into the fear for which I had inadvertently primed them, so that by July, a month before our trip, they were desperate not to go.

Not going was not an option. It was my mother's birthday, her eightieth, and my sister Linda was throwing her a party. It was a homecoming celebration too, my mother's return to Chicago after a ten-year absence. The passing of my father had triggered in her a sense of wanderlust, which she satisfied with six years in Maryland followed by four in Orlando. I had happily supported those moves.

Not only had they eliminated our obligation to visit my native city, which had just begun to make its push to be the nation's murder capital, but Maryland, with its proximity to D.C., and Orlando, with its Harry Potter theme park, were excellent places to vacation with kids. But then my mother's health declined, and Linda convinced her to come back home, to the South Side, to be exact, where there was an assisted-living facility capable of meeting her medical and financial needs. Who could argue with that? I could, and did, when I learned the facility was located in an area nearly mythic for its dangers. I called my mother and urged her to reconsider.

"What's to reconsider?" she asked. "Linda looked everywhere and this is the only place she could find."

"But the neighborhood's not safe."

"It's not safe anywhere," she replied.

"Of course it is."

"No it isn't. You could choke on a chicken bone tonight and die in your own kitchen."

"I like my chances of that not happening."

"And I," she said, "like putting my trust in God. You *do* still believe in God, don't you?"

It was a rhetorical question, designed to bring the conversation to an end. A moment later I revived it, this time with Linda, imploring her to find a different facility. "What's wrong with this one?" she asked. "Did you even look at the link I sent you?"

I had. The building was a high-rise on well-kept grounds, including a spacious patio where residents played board games and took meals, situated behind a six-foot metal security fence. Interior photos were of spacious apartments and smiling medical staff helping the elderly to walk and navigate stairs. There was a recreational room and a cafeteria. A security desk abutted the front door.

If the property itself had been the only consideration, I would have risen from my computer pleased as punch. Instead, I typed the address into Google Maps and took a virtual tour of the neighborhood, moving the cursor for blocks in all directions until I had my fill of graffiti, taverns, boarded up businesses, garbage-littered lots, liquor stores, and groups of men, their images frozen—I allowed myself to imagine, just to fully embody the spirit of my objection—right before weapons were drawn. "The facility isn't the problem," I said. "It's the neighborhood."

"The neighborhood? What's wrong with it?"

"It's not safe."

She snorted. "Tell me somewhere that is."

"*Here*," I said. "The house I'm in right now is *safe*. The neighborhood is *safe*. There are no murderers, no drug epidemic, no gangs, no drive-by shootings."

"Are there chicken bones?" she asked.

Thus concluded that conversation too. Later, I revived it once more, only this time alone. The clock on the nightstand glowed 3:12 a.m., not an uncommon hour to find me awake, working through some perturbation. I was trying to wrap my head around becoming so accustomed to violence that you assumed it was everywhere, and its forms included everything. Perhaps it was a subconscious survival strategy, a process of convincing yourself that the conditions in which you lived were, by and large, manageable, for people everywhere managed them, and of accepting that sometimes the conditions prevailed, for people everywhere died. Death by gun or chicken bone; what matter the means if the end was the same? I supposed I had been inculcated in a strand of that philosophy too, since it had not occurred to me that the South Side was uniquely dangerous until I had moved away. And now my mother, on the eve of her return, was trying to psych herself into believing her demise was as likely to come from a bird as a bullet.

I decided we could use some psyching out too, a way of shifting the concern of physical harm from our itinerary's core to its periphery. Our plan was to fly in and out of Chicago in a single day; we would change that to a week. We would stay at a high-end hotel downtown and spend six days as carefree tourists. I discussed this idea with Brenda the next morning, and soon afterward she and the boys were perusing tourists' websites, gleefully making lists of museums, historic landmarks, and the best restaurants for deep-dish pizza. This continued for several days, so we might have departed in high spirits had Dorian, the day before we left, not mentioned the trip to a friend. "*Chicago?*" the friend exclaimed. "I hope you don't *get shot!*"

A third of the city's 2.7 million residents lived on the South Side, and ninety-three percent of them were black. They occupied an expanse of land spanning 828 square miles, larger than most major American cities, making it possible to drive for hours and see only people of color. I was personally familiar with this demographic, of course, and yet after being away for so long it was surreal to experience, particularly coming on the heels of our week downtown, where racial diversity was abundant, albeit in a segregated sort of way. Which was to say the housekeepers, doormen, bus drivers, meter maids, and museum staff were almost exclusively black, and the tourists were almost exclusively not. It reminded me of being back in Boston, where there was always such a scarcity of black patrons in places like art galleries and theaters that I would catch myself exclaiming *There's one* whenever one came into view. Now, as we drove into the heart of the

South Side, I played this game again, searching for whites instead.

Meanwhile, the boys were in the back seat, silently watching their luck run out. A lot of good being raised outside of a ghetto did them now, they were probably thinking, though they could have been worrying more specifically about reuniting with their extended kin. It was how I had felt when visiting my aunts and uncles, whose children, for the most part, were on the fast-track to morgues and prisons. This was true of two cousins in particular, with their flamboyant style of dress, their swearing and smoking, their propensity for drinking wine from bottles and boasting of the hustles they had mastered. It was these two cousins who introduced one of my older brothers to pot and alcohol, who in turn introduced them to my twin brother and me, and we, in turn, despite being or because we were only fourteen, decided to make getting wasted our life's pursuit. But at least my sons would not be with their cousins for very long—not that it had taken very long, I reminded myself, at a family gathering many years ago when someone coaxed Adrian to drink some beer. He was three.

"How much longer?" Adrian asked now.

Brenda checked the GPS on her phone. "About forty minutes."

Dorian asked, "And how long are we staying again?"

"A few hours," Brenda replied. "Four, five tops."

"*That* long?" he said.

The car fell silent again. Outside, the Google Maps app I had navigated played out in 3-D; block after block of bleak inner-city landscape, complete with liquor stores on nearly every corner, flanked by loitering males. When we stopped at red lights, I paid special attention to the loiterers who eyed our car, recalling a time when Brenda and I saw a man smash the passenger window of the driver idling next to us and snatch her purse from the seat. I had hit the gas, barreling wildly through the intersection, my desire to assist the woman overwhelmed by a need to flee. Now I glanced to my right; Brenda's purse was on the floor, safely out of reach. We could still be car-jacked, though—our rented yellow SUV with Missouri plates seemed to encourage it. But my real concern was random gunfire, because a part of me did not think it would be random at all. It would be destiny, a karmic correction of an oversight that occurred thirty years prior.

It was 1985. My infatuation with pot and alcohol had run its course, and now I was twenty-one with an appetite for cocaine. One night, while en route to pick up a gram on credit from a dealer friend, I no sooner entered the alley that led to his apartment complex than a man stepped from the shadows and put a gun to my head. His free hand searched my pockets, and then, finding nothing, the armed one motioned me toward the stairs. I went to the third floor. After my friend answered his door and gave me the dope, I told him what had happened, and we shared a good laugh about it, for that was how commonplace these things were. Thirty minutes later, my friend was found dead where I had stood at gunpoint, his body filled with six bullets, at least one of which, I always believed, was intended for me. I had not shared that story with my sons. I was not sure I would. But I thought of it often. I thought of it every time I told them how lucky they were, just to remind myself that I, in my own way, had been lucky too.

"How much longer now?" Dorian asked.

Brenda checked the GPS. "Fourteen minutes."

"I don't think I'm going to make it," he said.

"Oh no," she replied, looking over her shoulder. "You're car sick?"

"Yes."

Brenda faced me. "We need to stop."

"*Stop?*"

"There," she said, pointing to a restaurant's parking lot.

So this is the karmic correction, I thought: *murdered in front of Harold's Chicken Shack while my son vomits on my shoes.* "I'm not stopping," I said.

"He's nauseous."

"It'll pass." I looked at him in the rearview mirror. "Crack your window, *boy.*"

"It *is* cracked."

"Just stop," Brenda persisted, "and let him walk around for a bit."

Dorian said, "I don't want to walk around."

"See?" I told her. "He's fine."

"I'm not fine. I just don't want to get shot."

"Me either," Adrian added.

"No one's getting shot," I assured them, surveying the area. I faced Brenda and asked, "Did you bring a bag?"

She rummaged through her purse for one of the plastic grocery bags she always brought for him when we went on long drives. But she did not have any.

"How could you not have any?"

"I just don't."

"Well, he can't throw up in a rental."

"Can he get shot in one?" Adrian asked.

Dorian burped.

"Roll down your window some more," Brenda instructed him.

"Not too much," I added.

Brenda said, "If he throws up it'll be your fault."

"No, it'll be *your* fault."

"Maybe it'll be Dorian's fault," Adrian offered, "for being sick."

No, it would be their mother's. She was the one, after all, who had wanted them to see how lucky *she* was to have been raised in a middle-class suburb. So before heading to the South Side, we had added an hour to the commute by driving twenty-five miles west of downtown to see her childhood house, and the houses of best friends, her middle school, and then her high school, where we stopped for her to take a photo in front of the marquee that read, "Welcome Back!" as if they had been expecting her. Every once in a while, one of the boys remarked about how nice everything was, and it was true. Clean streets. Immaculate houses. Lawns neat as putting greens. Pedestrians waving to us as we passed. I did not wave back, as I was too busy being jealous. With a start in life like this, I could have been anything. I was doing all right as a college professor, sure, but it was not as if I taught at Harvard, or held an endowed chair. And what of my personality? There was an inner-city intensity to it, an edge sharp enough to cut steel. Then there was the constant feeling I had of being slighted somehow, *punked*, and I would be damned if I let that happen.

Take that incident with my brother-in-law, Rob, for instance, whose house was the final stop of our suburban tour. When Brenda and I first started dating, he warned me not to mistreat her. He was only doing what he thought was expected of him, Brenda assured me, and I assured her I was only doing what was expected of me when I threatened to kick his ass. That was all South Side speaking, most likely, the ghetto in me that asserted itself at the slightest provocation. Even as we had pulled away from Brenda's high school, it took great restraint when a teenager stepped in front of our car, peering down at his phone rather than heeding the Do Not Walk sign, for me not to lay into my horn. If I had been raised in this suburb, I bet I would have only thought to toot it.

"What's up, what's up, *what's up?*" That was Rob. We were standing in his driveway, our car idling to emphasize our hurry. He shook my hand and asked, "How're things popping?"

"Things are popping," I replied, "fairly well."

He hugged his little sister, then turned his attention to his nephews, whom he had not seen since they were toddlers. "Look at these *Gs!*" he exclaimed. "They're full-grown *gangstas,* like me!"

He was, actually, a cook. He was also consistent; for as long as I had known him, he acted as if he had been born in a housing project and quit school when he was four. Spending his formative years in a middle-class suburb, which happened to be overwhelmingly white, had obviously raised difficult questions for him about what it meant to be black, and he had found the answers in rap videos. I had met many young men like him in college, especially in my African American literature classes, where more often than not they sat in the back row, looking very upset. Remembering them now, and watching Rob throw slow-motion jabs at my sons' bellies, the jealously I felt at not being raised here waned a little. At least, as far as being a brother-from-the-hood was concerned, I was the real deal. And my sons, once I expanded the range of my stories, would know what that meant beyond the stereotypes.

The suburb was now a couple of hours behind us, and my mother's new residence, according to the GPS, was only minutes away. Relief descended on me, tinged with shame. We would make it without incident, and it seemed foolish to have been so concerned. I had taken the warped view of the world being unsafe and narrowed its scope to a mere speck of human existence, which was to say, me. Destiny? Karmic correction? Give me a break. I faced Dorian and asked, "How do you feel, son?"

"Sick," he said.

Adrian rested a hand on his shoulder. "But at least you're alive."

There it was, straight ahead—the building I had seen on Google Maps, towering above a sign that read, "Church View." There was in fact a church within view, though without sacrificing accuracy they could have named the facility "See Failed Businesses," as a trail of closed stores stretched the entire opposite block. The street running parallel to it was busy with traffic, suggesting a time when commerce boomed and this was not simply a pass-through. Other than the steady flow of vehicles, the only evidence of life was a woman with an infant waiting at a bus stop.

Brenda pointed out a parking lot adjacent to my mother's building, but it was gated, and there was no attendant in the booth. I circled the block until I found an open spot on the street, not far from the building's entrance, directly across from the patio. The patio was crowded with people I now recognized as relatives, including two of my brothers and old family friends. I turned off the car and said, with a fair amount of sincerity, "Let's have some fun." I was happy to see my siblings and mother, of course, as well as to have the boys spend time with them, but I knew the main form of entertainment, as it had been at parties I attended like this as a child, would be booze.

And so it was. We did not let the boys out of our sight, which they made easy for us, offering perfunctory greet-

ings to everyone before joining us at one of the tables in
the recreational room. My mother, sitting next to me, was
in full bloom as the honoree, dividing her time between
accepting hugs and gifts and dancing to the R&B oldies
that Linda, acting as DJ, blared through the room. At one
point we went to see my mother's apartment, but otherwise we drifted from table to table, making small talk.
Four hours in, as night started to fall, I told Brenda and
the boys it was time, and we began saying our goodbyes.
But before we got far my twin appeared at my side. "Let's
make a run," he said.

"Do what?"

"Make *a run*," he repeated, by way of clarification.

"Can't. We're about to leave."

"You can't *leave*," he protested. "You *just* got here."

"We've got this early flight tomorrow and . . ."

"Come on, bro," he said, smiling. "I haven't seen you
in, *hell*, I don't even know how long. You can't have one
last beer?"

I glanced at Brenda. She was giving me a look that
said *Of course* or *Say yes and I'll kill you.* Twenty-one years of
marriage and I still got those confused.

"Sure," I told Jim. "I'll have one more beer."

"None left," he responded. "That's why we have to
make a run."

A cousin was walking by but stopped when he heard
us. "Y'all making a run?"

"Yeah," Jim replied.

"Where to?"

"Liquor store down the street."

"Down the street?" I said. "We're *walking*?"

"I'll walk with y'all," the cousin offered.

My childhood friend Paul, seated at an adjacent table,
said, "I'll walk too."

There was no way I was walking to a liquor store in that neighborhood, especially not at night . . . and then I saw it, a flicker of a smirk on Jim's lips. He thought I was afraid—Linda must have told him what I said about the area being unsafe!—and was preparing to tease me if I declined. So I knew I had to go. I fell in step with him and the others as they moved through the room. When we reached the door, I looked back at Brenda and the boys; each face was a copy of the others' horrified expression.

The first time I made a beer-run I was fifteen. The proprietor of the store was a Middle-Eastern man who never asked for ID. He would simply slip the liquor into a white McDonald's bag and send you on your way, sometimes calling out a reminder, as you were leaving, that you had not made the purchase there. People would sometimes forget that under duress, though, and tell their arresting officer the truth, and one day you would show up at the store to find it closed by order of police. It was always only a matter of time before it opened again with a sign proclaiming new ownership, and it would be a different Middle-Eastern man inside, packing liquor for underage customers in white McDonald's bags. I half expected that ritual to play out with the Middle-Eastern man serving us now, even though I was far from being fifteen, and this was not that store.

This store, in fact, was less a store than a small vault. The four of us could barely fit inside the twenty-five-square-foot enclosure made from floor to ceiling of bullet-proof glass. There had been no one there when we arrived, so we knocked on the glass until the man appeared on the other side of it from a back room. We told him what we wanted. He disappeared and returned a moment later

with two six-packs of malt liquor. He put them into a Lazy
Susan, waiting to spin the opened end toward us until
our money had been inserted in a slot in the glass. As we
turned to leave, I thought, *I did not buy it here.*

The sun was low in the sky; in a few minutes it would
be dark. When we left my mother's building a half hour
ago, the thought of being out here in the dark could have
given me hives. I had even started walking quickly as soon
as we were outside, though I checked myself after a few
steps. A fast stride could be interpreted as a sign of fear,
and showing fear in the ghetto was a mistake, even if it
were only of being late for an appointment. *Hell if I care
if I'm late* was the message you wanted to send, and often,
in my younger days, I had emphasized that point by pausing to smoke a cigarette, or to retie my shoe. A slow stride
said you were a bad ass, someone not to be messed with
or punked. I remembered how after the man had put the
gun to my head, I had walked slowly up the stairs to get
the coke, and when I returned I walked slowly away. I bet
my friend's final steps were slow ones.

I wondered what Brenda and the boys were doing.
They were worried sick about me, no doubt, and while
I was in the store waiting for our beer I had thought to
send them a text, telling them not to be. It was all coming
back to me now, how to be at ease on these streets, how to
gracefully surf the danger like a wave beneath your board.
Besides, there were no waves here—the block between
the store and the assisted-living facility was empty, not a
soul for anyone to be concerned about except for my bad
ass self . . .

"You alright?" Jim asked.

"I'm fine," I said. "Why?"

"You walking all slow and shit."

"Hell if I care," I said.

He smiled, as if acknowledging the return of the old me; the me who had run the streets with him and our friends; the me who dropped out of high school at sixteen and spent most of my days and nights getting high; the me before my friend's murder shook me to my core, forcing me to rethink my choices in a way nothing else had or could. I swore off drugs that night, and soon afterward moved from the South Side and returned to school, and now I was back here again, in the heart of the ghetto, on a beer-run like so often before. A wish suddenly rose in me that I had never left, that I had been living here all this time despite the violence, but I dismissed it as a mirage, a trick of a nostalgic mind, even before I saw the four men.

They were across the street, coming our way, and they, too, walked slowly. There was no misfit in their group, though, meaning no one dressed as I was in Birkenstocks, cargo shorts, and a REI t-shirt with snow-capped mountains. Like Jim, our cousin, and Paul, they wore sneakers, baggy jeans and t-shirts loose enough to conceal weapons.

Oblivious to their approach, Jim was saying something about remodeling his basement. Or maybe he was not oblivious at all—how could he be?—and talking about his basement was a ruse intended to sidestep a confrontation. I nodded, pretending to listen, and in that way I hoped we signaled that we were discussing important matters and not out for trouble. I looked toward the men once more. They were crossing the street, headed right for us. Then they were there.

The one in front, wearing a black do-rag and a noose of gold chains, made the first move. "How you brothers doing?" he asked.

"We making it, cuz," Jim said. "We making it." Similar greetings were exchanged, without anyone breaking stride, and then the men were behind us, and we were behind them, and Jim was talking about his floors. "I want to go with hardwood," he was saying, "but that shit's kind of expensive. So it'll probably have to be carpet. Actually, I think maybe I'll just paint."

I nodded again, as if affirming his decision, rather than the broad truth of that encounter, its humanity that, more than the violence, had defined my life in the ghetto. And this gentle reminder of that fact was destiny, the karmic correction of an oversight long overdue—that was how I would come to think of it, at least, during the drive back to the hotel, when I told the boys this story.

RACE STORIES

Once a year my college hosts a dinner for its faculty of color. There are not many of us, so the gatherings are small, allowing for full participation in discussions we have after settling around the table. Various topics are covered, from how to handle disruptive students to how to grow orchids, though invariably, at some point, we turn to race. It happens this time when the Vice President for Diversity and Inclusion, our hostess, rises and says, "A short time ago, while on his way to this very dinner, Jerald was involved in an altercation." All eyes focus on me. I nod, confirming that it is true, and then continue slicing my braised potato.

It is not my style to rush a good race story. They are becoming increasingly rare, it seems to me, and when I attend cocktail parties, or simply socialize with friends, I find myself resorting to familiar tropes; security guards following me at malls; white women removing purses from grocery carts upon my approach; state troopers trailing my car, hoping to catch a miscue. Better to speak about the events that of late permeate the evening news, namely police killings of unarmed black men, but after a while they make me depressed, and I fret over my teenage sons. The stories I favor are not only upsetting but also uplifting; they are rich with irony and tinged with humor; they are unique, in some way, and lend themselves to interesting digressions, and their protagonists always confront villains, even if not always with success—when I come into a race story with these components, I prefer to delay its telling, allowing it to breathe, so to speak, like a newly uncorked Merlot.

"I was coming from my office," I begin, after having a sip of iced tea. I slice more potato, eat a piece, and then place my knife and fork on my plate. "It's just across the street, as I think most of you know, but it still took a while to get here because I left as classes were changing." Everyone is familiar with the college's racial demographic, so rather than reference it I merely pause to let the image sink in of a middle-aged black man in a throng of white students. I do note, however, since the college's security force is comparatively diverse, that it was a white guard in the lobby downstairs who stopped me.

"Stopped you?" someone asks. "For what?"

"For," I explain, "looking shady."

"*Shady*? The guard *said* that to you?"

"Not directly. Her impression was relayed to me by the security guard who subsequently came for my arrest." I face the Vice President and ask, "She did say 'shady,' didn't she?"

"Actually," the Vice President responds, "I believe she said 'suspicious.'"

The room erupts. My colleagues are outraged, as well they should be. I do not look shady or suspicious. I look professorial, perhaps never more so than today, since the new herringbone sport coat I am wearing has leather patches on the elbows, which perfectly match my leather satchel. But the security guard was not buying it. And I, at first, was not buying that I was the object of her attention. There was a good chance, I reasoned, that her *Stop right there!* was directed at one of the several dozen students passing through the lobby. So I ignored her.

The guard called out again, this time including, *You in the sport coat!* before asking why I was in the building. I had made it halfway up the flight of stairs behind her desk, and now, as I stopped, students flowed around me, showing no interest in my detainment. Perhaps they, like the security guard, thought it perfectly fine for a black male to be made to account for his presence, regardless of where it was, and regardless of his attire. Regardless, even, of the possibility that he was not naturally inclined to account for anything. I faced her and asked, "Why are you singling me out?"

"Because," she responded, "*I can.* What are you doing in here?"

It was, on its surface, a reasonable question. My college is in the heart of Boston, located in an area once so saturated with crime that it had been dubbed The Combat Zone. In its heyday, during the sixties and seventies, one came here to visit the strip clubs and peep shows, or to hire prostitutes, or to buy dope, or to prey upon the connoisseurs of these vices, often violently, sometimes fatally. Many of these connoisseurs were enlisted servicemen, on leave from the Boston Navy Yard, and because they were still in uniform there was occasionally the impression that a military operation was afoot, a battle being waged, that this was, in fact, a place of war.

For the residents of neighboring Chinatown, it was. Despite efforts of the police to restrict the debauchery to within a certain radius, spillover was inevitable. And sometimes the spillover became a surge, when drunken servicemen poured into the neighborhood, looking to attack the communist Chinese or Vietcong, for which any Asian American would do. For years the residents of Chinatown protested the sanctioned existence of The Combat Zone, often marching with handmade signs in front of the X-rated movie theaters and sex merchandise stores, and holding candlelight vigils, until finally, in the mid-80s, the city relented. Urban renewal projects resulted in most of the adult businesses being replaced by luxury apartment complexes, four-star hotels, and high-end bars. My college relocated here from across town in the 1990s. By then The Combat Zone was a far cry from what it once was, and yet remnants of its past remained, as they still do.

We are often reminded of this. Our college's police chief routinely sends emails urging us to be on high alert because a member of our community was robbed on campus. There are warnings against traveling alone after dark. Sometimes we are informed of crimes that did not involve us but had occurred in the vicinity, usually a block west, where addicts, alcoholics, and ex-convicts loiter in front of a homeless shelter. Most of these loiterers are black males, it is true; one could imagine some junkie among them entering a campus building in hopes of swiping an unattended laptop or iPhone. One could also imagine him, upon being stopped by security, making a mad dash for the door. I, when stopped, did not make a mad dash for the door; matching satchel and elbow patches notwithstanding, my failure to flee should have signaled to the guard I was not one of those men. And so when she asked me a second time what I was doing in the building, I sent a clearer signal. "You have no right to ask me that," I told her.

Wide-eyed, she sprang from her stool and ordered me to produce college identification or to leave at once. But having worked at the college for five years, the last three of which as department chair, I was familiar with many of its policies and procedures, notably the one that said anyone entering a campus building after 6:00 p.m. was required to show identification—but not before. It was an hour before. "When you ask all of these people walking past you to show IDs," I said, "I'll show you mine."

"I don't *need* to ask them for their IDs," she snapped, "because I *recognize* them."

"All of them?"

"Every single one!" She reached for the phone on her desk. "I'm *warning* you, either show college ID, or get out of here!"

Now some students did pause to take note of what was happening, and it occurred to me that a few of mine might be among them. I did not want to be a spectacle for my students, at least no longer than necessary, and decided to leave. Besides, once I filed a complaint the security guard would likely lose her job, and I would subsequently make good use of a story about being racially profiled while en route to a racially profiled dinner. I smiled at my good fortune as I climbed the stairs. Behind me, I could hear the guard shouting into her phone, summoning reinforcements.

The reinforcements, as it turned out, was a single security guard, this time African American. When she approached the dining room, I was standing outside its door with the Vice President, having just recounted my altercation. The guard introduced herself to us and said, "I'm sorry to bother you, but I received a report"— here she produced a small notepad and drew it close to her face—"of a middle-aged black male, medium build, approximately five-ten, close-cropped hair, and looking, um, suspicious."

The Vice President rested a hand on my shoulder. "I believe this is your man."

"Good evening," I said. "I'm Professor Walker."

The guard slapped her forehead.

"Literally *slapped* it," I say to my colleagues, and then the Vice President and I burst into laughter, as we did when it happened. Some of our colleagues join us, while others call for an investigation, a protest, an apology, even a sit-in, and then someone raises his voice above the others to say he was stopped in the lobby by that security guard too. He is black, and then another black male says it also happened to him, and another. The main difference between their experiences and mine is that when the security guard demanded identification, they produced it, concerned, perhaps, for their safety, maybe even for their lives. I understand that. I respect it. Everyone knows how race stories like these begin, after all. But we do not know how they will end.

ADVICE TO A FAMILY MAN

You are on Amtrak's regional from New York to Boston editing a student's essay when your pencil slips from your hand, lands on the adjacent seat, and rolls under its passenger's right buttock. Only the eraser remains visible, and not all of it at that, just a centimeter or so, though that's enough, you think, to be pinched free. Give the consequences of a mishap serious consideration, however, since the passenger is female, and white no less. She's in her twenties, thin, blonde, and has large blue eyes, but you are speculating about her eyes because they are closed, as the woman is asleep. Her head rests on a bunched-up sweater pressed against the window, her body angled away from yours, which is why her ass is partially airborne and you are imagining a scenario whereby it descends, suddenly, onto your forefinger and thumb.

. . . *Upon feeling something wiggle beneath her, the woman wakes to see you snatch back your hand. She screams, causing passengers to rise from their seats to look your way, including the three members of your family. Your first thought is if you'd sat with one of them this wouldn't be happening, but when you entered the car it was already crowded with only scattered seats remaining. Your fifteen-year-old is directly in front of you, your seventeen-year-old is directly in front of him, and your wife is farther down the car. When she pinpoints the source of the scream, she weaves through the passengers now gathered in the aisle, reaching your side as the woman accuses you of groping her.*

Swear you are no groper. Say you are a family man traveling, this very instance, with your wife and sons. Vouch for your character further by mentioning you are returning from seeing three Broadway musicals in three days, but given the cost of Broadway musicals some passengers look to be as skeptical of this as you were when your wife said the tickets were on sale. One of these skeptics calls for security, a member of which just happens to be entering the car, and who just happens to be black. Rather than take comfort in his race, however, be put-off by his comportment—his upturned chin, for instance, and his pompous sneer—and decide that in the olden days he would have been a house slave, the kind who despised his brethren in the field, where you undoubtedly would have been.

When he reaches you, explain what happened. He lowers his chin and says, "So let me make sure I'm understanding you correctly. You lost control of your pencil, it fell down, *and then* landed up under *this lady's rear?"*

Here your fifteen-year-old, who of late has made a habit of contradicting you, says, "Wouldn't that defy the laws of gravity?"

The security guard nods at him. "So you see where I'm going with this?"

"My husband isn't a pervert," your wife interjects, at last rising to your defense. "He's just a goofball and a klutz."

Your seventeen-year-old agrees and offers proof. "That's why when we were in the airport last year," he explains, "he went into the ladies' restroom" . . .

Rethink that verb. *Went* implies a deliberate act with forethought and perhaps even malicious intent. You should have used *wandered*, which is more in line with the truth of what happened; you were reading a text instead of the bathroom's gender designation. By the time you looked up from your phone, you were standing before a row of stalls with nary a urinal in sight. Instead of recognizing this clue for what it was and abruptly leaving, you proceeded to do your business, rejoicing at the thought that someone had finally designed a men's room with an eye toward discretion. Having a full bladder, in your estimation, is insufficient reason for men to hold their penises in public spaces mere inches from other men holding their penises without a substantial partition between them, especially since, should one of these men wink at you while stepping back from the urinal, you might have an unobstructed view of a penis in service of something other than a bladder. The man who recently did this, you'd wager, had not arrived at the urinal next to yours by wandering.

. . . *"I* wandered *into the ladies' restroom,"* you say, *"while reading a text."*

"And yet," your *fifteen-year-old responds, "you* stayed *in there, even though there were no urinals."*

"But there were no women either," counters your seventeen-year-old. *"Not like that time last month at his college."* . . .

Technically speaking, there were no *women* in that restroom either, but rather a *woman,* a close friend of yours, fortunately, for who knows what would have happened had a stranger exited a stall to see you at the sink washing your hands. After saying hello, your friend strolled to the sink next to yours and turned on the faucet. "You do realize," she said, pumping the soap dispenser, "that this is a ladies' room?"

"So I've gathered," you replied.

"Then why, if you don't mind my asking, are you in here?"

"I've obviously made a mistake."

"To be perfectly honest," she said, "it's not obvious. Because assuming you didn't see the image of the woman on the door, *in a skirt*—"

"—And I didn't—"

"—okay, assuming that, it would be difficult for someone not to notice, once they're in here, that there are only stalls."

"Which was all I was looking for," you said, resting a hand on your belly. "Bad sushi last night."

Later that day, however, when you told your family what happened, your fifteen-year-old noted that he'd eaten the same sushi and felt fine. You might as well have claimed a group of women pulled you inside the restroom and held you captive, since that would have been just as unbelievable, even though something similar actually occurred to you when you were nine. While zigzagging through the halls of your elementary school, your attention on the black and white tiles as you pretended to be a human checker, you looked up to see a half-dozen teenaged girls bearing down on you. Two of them suddenly grabbed your arms and another cupped your mouth, their actions swift and coordinated enough to suggest the plan was long in the making, though you understood it not to have been after they'd ushered you into the girls' bathroom and one of them asked, "Now what?" No one had an answer. They thought the matter through while grooming themselves in the mirror and smoking cigarettes. Meanwhile, you stood against the far wall trying not to cry, which made your wails all the more pronounced when they finally erupted. Your captors rushed to your side, each taking turns giving you a hug and telling you that everything was okay, but you believed otherwise because if there were a greater evil than a boy being in a girls' bathroom, it had not been made known to you. And then it was made known to you; one of the girls, after escorting you to the door, kissed your cheek.

Perhaps it is the nature of fifteen-year-old boys in general, and not yours specifically, to contradict your view of things, for when you informed your older brother of that age what happened he told you to count your blessings. After that you felt less tormented by the incident. Indeed, when you reached puberty, you longed for its reenactment, though no amount of time spent loitering near girls' bathrooms could bring it forth. So you settled for its memory, which always brought a smile to your face and occasionally, four and a half decades later, still does. But remembering it now on the train, do not smile, for it has just occurred to you that perhaps, on some subconscious level, your recent excursions into women's bathrooms are linked to that incident. Maybe you are more than just a goofball and a klutz. Which would mean, by logical extension, that your pencil slipping from your hand to land where it landed was no accident. Do you see where you're going with this?

You do. And you don't like it. Stay out of your head. Retrieve your pencil, as any family man would do, but first, as a matter of prudence, check to see if the woman is still asleep. She is. And she remains so until your fingers are an inch from the eraser, which is to say an inch from her right buttock. Her eyes, just as you'd speculated, are blue and large. As they grow larger, stammer, "I, um, I dropped my . . . um." Point to the thing you are trying to say. The woman glances down, sees and picks up the pencil. She smiles as she hands it to you. Thank her. Return your attention to your student's essay. Only pretend to be editing it, though, because you are already back in your head again.

Your train has arrived in Boston. As you make your way through the aisle, notice a half-dozen women approaching from the opposite direction. There is no one else in the car, only you and these women, and midway between you and them is a ladies' room. Your wife calls your name. Look to your left to see her and your sons. They are already on the platform, gesturing through the window for you to join them. "Let's go," your wife says, and your seventeen-year-old adds, "Daddy, come on." But then your fifteen-year-old responds, "He won't come," which, of course, is a contradiction. Because before he spoke, you were already at their side.

ACKNOWLEDGMENTS

I would like to thank 21st Century Essays series editors, Patrick Madden and David Lazar, for providing a home for essayists. I owe a tremendous debt to Steven Church and *The Normal School* magazine staff for their assistance with an earlier version of this book, and an even greater debt to my editor Kristen Elias Rowley and the Mad Creek Books staff for the final version's polish and shine. I'm enormously grateful to the National Endowment for the Arts for their timely fellowship, and to Emerson College for a much-needed sabbatical. A heartful thank you to Johnny Skoyles, Maria Flook, Lundy Braun, and John Trimbur for their valuable feedback and trusted friendship. Most of all, I am indebted to my brilliant wife, Brenda Molife, for being my first, middle, last, and best reader, and our wonderful sons, Adrian and Dorian, for their boundless love, inspiration, and material.

These essays originally appeared, sometimes in different form, in the following publications: "Unprepared" and "The Designated Driver," *The Harvard Review*; "Wars," *The Austin Review* (as "Milo"); "How to Make a Slave," *Southern Humanities Review*; "Dragon Slayers," *The Iowa Review*; "Breathe," *The New England Review*; "The Heart" and "Kaleshion," *Creative Nonfiction*; "Before Grief," *The Best African American Essays 2010*; "The Heritage Room," *Apogee*; "Feeding Pigeons," *Outsmart*; "Inauguration," "Balling," and "Race Stories," *The Normal School*; "Testimony," *The Saint Ann's Review*; "Thieves," *River Teeth*; "Simple," *Memoir*; "Advice to a Family Man," *Speculative Nonfiction* (as "Advice to an Honorable Man"); "Smoke," *New Ohio Review*.

"Dragon Slayers" was selected by David Foster Wallace for *The Best American Essays 2007*.

"Unprepared" was selected by Edwidge Danticat for *The Best American Essays 2011*.

"How to Make a Slave" was selected by Jeremiah Sullivan for *The Best American Essays 2014*.

"Breathe" was selected by Andre Aciman for *The Best American Essays 2020*.

ABOUT THE AUTHOR

Jerald Walker is the author of *The World in Flames: A Black Boyhood in a White Supremacist Doomsday Cult* and *Street Shadows: A Memoir of Race, Rebellion, and Redemption,* winner of the 2011 PEN New England Award for Nonfiction. He has published in magazines such as *Creative Nonfiction, Harvard Review, Missouri Review, River Teeth, Mother Jones, Iowa Review,* and *Oxford American,* and he has been widely anthologized, including five times in *The Best American Essays.* The recipient of James A. Michener and National Endowment for the Arts fellowships, Walker is a Professor of Creative Writing at Emerson College.

21st CENTURY ESSAYS
David Lazar and Patrick Madden, Series Editors

This series from Mad Creek Books is a vehicle to discover, publish, and promote some of the most daring, ingenious, and artistic nonfiction. This is the first and only major series that announces its focus on the essay—a genre whose plasticity, timelessness, popularity, and centrality to nonfiction writing make it especially important in the field of nonfiction literature. In addition to publishing the most interesting and innovative books of essays by American writers, the series publishes extraordinary international essayists and reprint works by neglected or forgotten essayists, voices that deserve to be heard, revived, and reprised. The series is a major addition to the possibilities of contemporary literary nonfiction, focusing on that central, frequently chimerical, and invariably supple form: The Essay.

How to Make a Slave and Other Essays
JERALD WALKER

Just an Ordinary Woman Breathing
JULIE MARIE WADE

My Private Lennon: Explorations from a Fan Who Never Screamed
SIBBIE O'SULLIVAN

*On Our Way Home from the Revolution: Reflections on Ukraine**
SONYA BILOCERKOWYCZ

Echo's Fugue
DESIRAE MATHERLY

This One Will Hurt You
PAUL CRENSHAW

The Trouble with Men: Reflections on Sex, Love, Marriage, Porn, and Power
DAVID SHIELDS

*Fear Icons: Essays**
KISHA LEWELLYN SCHLEGEL

Sustainability: A Love Story
NICOLE WALKER

Hummingbirds Between the Pages
CHRIS ARTHUR

*Annual Gournay Prize Winner

Love's Long Line
SOPHFRONIA SCOTT

The Real Life of the Parthenon
PATRICIA VIGDERMAN

You, Me, and the Violence
CATHERINE TAYLOR

Curiouser and Curiouser: Essays
NICHOLAS DELBANCO

Don't Come Back
LINA MARÍA FERREIRA CABEZA-VANEGAS

A Mother's Tale
PHILLIP LOPATE